MUSIC IN THE HIGH SCHOOL
Current Approaches to Secondary General Music Instruction

**Proceedings of the National Conference on
Music/Arts for the High School General Student
June 25–28, 1986, Orlando, Florida**

Edited by Timothy Gerber, The Ohio State University, Columbus, and
William O. Hughes, Florida State University, Tallahassee

Sponsored by
Music Educators National Conference and Florida State University, Tallahassee

Table of Contents

Table of Contents
(continued)

Foreword

Since the beginning of public school music instruction in America, a goal of music education has been to produce a musically enlightened, musically participatory adult society. *A Trend of High School Offerings and Enrollments: 1972-73 and 1981-82* by the National Center for Educational Statistics reported that from 1981 to 1982, only 22 percent of the nation's secondary school students were enrolled in music. The study also revealed that more high schools in this country offered band and choir instruction than any other music subject. Very few high schools offered any kind of music instruction for the nonperformer. For those students who could not qualify for band or choir, as well as for those who wanted to take nonperformance music courses, nothing was available.

According to *Arts, Education, and the States* by the Council of Chief State School Officers, twenty-two states now require at least one course in the arts for high school graduation. This requirement has motivated a number of high schools throughout the country to expand course offerings in music. With MENC's adoption of the 1990 goals (that every student K-12 have access to music instruction, that every high school require at least one course in the arts for graduation, and that all colleges require a course in the arts for admission), the number of states with arts requirements will surely increase, creating a critical need for nonperformance high school music courses.

If high school general music (or music for the nonperformer) is to become a meaningful option for high school students across the nation, serious questions must be addressed. What should be the content of these courses? How can high school students be motivated to study music in a general studies curriculum? Who will teach these courses? What specific teacher competencies are required for effective teaching of these courses?

These and other pertinent questions and issues provided impetus for The 1986 National Conference on Music/Arts for the High School General Student, held June 25–28 in Orlando, Florida. The conference was sponsored by MENC, the Society for General Music, and the Florida State University School of Music with assistance from the Florida Department of Education. Affiliate sponsors were Holt, Rinehart and Winston; Macmillan; the Orange County (Florida) Schools; Rhythm Band, Inc.; and Silver Burdett. A major goal of the conference was to stimulate dialogue on the issues facing general music teachers and to seek beginnings for eventual answers to the questions.

The conference attracted over eighty registrants from twenty-three states representing secondary school music teachers, elementary school music teachers, music supervisors, school board members, and college music education instructors and administrators. Participants were involved in an intensive schedule of keynote addresses, workshops, discussion groups, presentation of curriculum models, and writing projects.

In his keynote address, MENC President Paul Lehman spoke about the MENC Goals for 1990 and the role that expanded high school music curricula must play if those goals are to be achieved. Timothy Gerber of Ohio State University addressed the characteristics of adolescence and the cultivation of musical taste. The issues were debated in discussion groups, and project writing teams considered curricular emphases for development of general music instruction. The three-fold task of these groups was to develop a plan to create a climate of acceptance for general music in the high school; develop a rationale for the formulation of objectives; and design sample objectives from which teaching strategies could emerge. Workshop leaders demonstrated strategies, and curriculum models from Fulton County, Georgia, and Baltimore County, Maryland, were presented, showing diverse approaches toward achieving similar goals. As Charles Hoffer adjourned the conference, he charged the participants to seize the opportunity to move music into the mainstream of the high school curriculum.

Participants left Orlando with a conviction that general music at the high school level could and must be effective. They were excited about the challenge and eager to serve as resource persons in their respective communities and states. Lehman said, "Sixteen years ago we [MENC] called for a vital musical culture and an enlightened musical public. Today, we have the opportunity to take a giant step in that direction. Let's take that step." The 1986 National Conference on Music/Arts for the High School General Student was an historic first step. Publication of the proceedings carries the work forward to educators not attending the Orlando conference. It is hoped that the research, discussion, and recommendations of this volume will assist educators in initiating attractive, quality high school general music programs that will enhance the lives of their students and those of future generations.

William Hughes
Conference co-chairperson
Professor of Music
Florida State University

June Hinckley
State Supervisor of Music
Florida Department of Education

Susan Kenney
Conference co-chairperson
Chairman, MENC Society
  for General Music

Part I:

Keynote Addresses

A Music Program for 2001

by Paul R. Lehman

In 1970 the MENC National Executive Board adopted a set of goals that called for the creation of a vital musical culture and an enlightened musical public in the United States. In 1984, in the face of a mixed pattern of progress in the lengthy, up-and-down struggle toward these noble but amorphous objectives, the Board adopted a set of more precise and more narrowly defined goals and set 1990 as the deadline for achieving them.

These goals can be summarized as follows: (1) By 1990, every student K-12 shall have access to music instruction in school; (2) by 1990, every high school shall require at least one Carnegie unit of credit in music, art, theater, or dance for graduation; and (3) by 1990, every college and university shall require at least one Carnegie unit of credit in music, art, theater, or dance for admission.

High school general music and the Goals for 1990

We're here today to discuss the one fundamental element that relates directly to each of these three goals: the expansion of instructional programs in music and the arts for the general student in the high school. None of these three goals can be achieved without significantly expanded opportunities for the general student to study music in the high school, and that's why I believe that this topic is so important.

By "general student," I mean the student who for lack of interest, ability, time, or for whatever reason, does not participate in the school's performing groups. Too often in today's high school there are no music courses available to this student.

A curriculum that locks out students

In most schools, students are locked out of the instrumental program unless they begin study in the elementary school. Many choral groups also require prerequisite study, even those that do not demand interest and ability in vocal music. As a result, the majority of high school students simply have no reasonable access to music. This unhappy circumstance is in direct violation of Goal 1, which calls for *every* student to have access to music instruction. The situation is not the fault of a conspiracy of school administrators; it is the fault of our own curriculum.

Goal 2 calls for all students to study the arts in high school. But this is just not possible unless we make music courses available to the general student. Music is the most popular of the arts. It's the one potentially most accessible to most students. It would be unthinkable to try to meet this requirement through courses in the other arts alone, excluding music.

Twenty-two states currently require at least one course in the arts for high school graduation. Seventeen of these have added the requirement since 1979. But the options that will satisfy the requirement vary enormously, and the situation is not nearly as good as it appears to be on the surface. We have a long way to go before a requirement limited to music, art, theater, and dance is universal, and we have an immense task ahead to provide the courses that will make it sustainable.

Goal 3 calls for colleges to require study of the arts for admission. This is simply not feasible until such study becomes generally available in high schools. Historically, high school graduation requirements and college admission requirements have moved hand in hand, with the leadership being provided sometimes by one and sometimes by the other. They can never diverge sharply, for political and economic reasons. Colleges cannot require something that schools don't offer.

The trend of the late eighties

I think that the expansion of general music into the high school represents the most important trend of the late 1980s in our profession, and I use the word "trend" advisedly. We've abused and debased the word "trend" to the point of meaninglessness by squandering it on even the most superficial fads. But I believe that here we have a genuine trend. At least I hope so. The next three years will tell us.

It is because this topic is so important that I want to thank Bill Hughes, Susan Kenney, June Hinckley, and all of their colleagues who have worked so hard to make this meeting possible. I also want to applaud the initiative of the Society for General Music and the Florida State University for responding to the need to do something concrete about this issue. It is clearly a topic that can no longer be ignored.

I have pointed out on other occasions that the students who entered the first grade last fall will graduate from college in the year 2001. Similarly, the high school class of 2001 will be entering preschool programs this fall and next and will enter the first grade in 1989. You and I owe it to the young people of America to put into place by 1990 in every elementary and secondary school in the nation, from Lake Okeechobee to Lake Wobegon, a balanced, comprehensive, and sequential program of high-quality music instruction taught by

4

qualified teachers. Unless we do this we are failing in our commitment to excellence, and we're certainly not meeting the needs of the class of 2001.

Basic components of a balanced high school program

Let us consider for a moment just what a balanced high school music program should consist of. In addition to an array of instrumental and vocal performing groups, it should also include varied offerings in music literature, history, theory, composition, or fine arts. The titles, of course, don't matter as much as the content. These courses usually will be suitable for the students in our performing groups as well, but most of them should be designed primarily for the general student population.

Large schools, of course, can offer a greater variety of courses than small schools, but even in the smallest school there should be at least one nonperformance offering, without prerequisites, available to every student every year, and it should be scheduled so as not to conflict with required single-section courses. It is perfectly all right to have a sequence of two or even three courses so that advanced study is possible, but there must always be something available to every student. By using computers, the repertoire of instructional alternatives available can be expanded enormously and individualized almost without limit.

General music, of course, has several meanings. It may refer to music for the general student population, or it may refer to general skills and knowledge in music as distinguished from specialized skills and knowledge. In this sense general music should be taught in every instructional setting, including high school performing groups. The Comprehensive Musicianship Program (CMP) was on the right track. Its principles are as sound today as they were in the 1960s. In every curricular setting we should be teaching skills and knowledge based broadly on the elements of music. Only the emphasis should vary from one setting to another.

I would like to organize the remainder of my remarks around four questions that relate to the four discussion groups that are to meet later in this conference: (1) What are the learning outcomes that should result from our offerings in general music? (2) How do we motivate the high school student in the general music class? (3) What is the impact of expanded high school general music offerings on the traditional high school music program? (4) What competencies are needed by teachers of high school general music?

Discussion group issues
Desired learning outcomes for general music courses

First, what are the learning outcomes that should result from our offerings in general music? According to MENC's landmark publication, *The School Music Program: Description and Standards*, the general music program should be designed to produce individuals who are able to make music alone and with others; are able to improvise and create music; are able to use music vocabulary and notation; are able to respond to music aesthetically, intellectually, and emotionally; are acquainted with a wide variety of music, including diverse musical styles and genres; understand the role music has played and continues to play in the lives of human beings; are able to make aesthetic judgments based on critical listening and analysis rather than on superficial stereotypes and shallow prejudices; have developed a commitment to music; support the musical life of the community and encourage others to do so; and are able to continue their musical learning independently.

These outcomes are as important, as useful, and as relevant for the secondary school as they are for the elementary school. Naturally, not every one of these objectives can be pursued in every course. But this list provides the menu of outcomes from which we can select the appetizers, the entrees, and the desserts for every course in music.

Let's not forget that at the high school level as well as the elementary level, learning in music is based on skills and knowledge. It's not based on merely having a good time. Musical learning should certainly be enjoyable, but the greatest enjoyment comes from solid achievement toward worthwhile goals. Our instruction should never be random or haphazard. It should always be focused. It should always seek to achieve specific, well-conceived outcomes defined in advance. And these should be outcomes that require every student to be actively involved rather than passively acquiescent.

Motivating students in general music classes

The second question is: How do we motivate the high school student in the general music class? Nothing is more important than motivation. Learning is based on motivation. Students learn what they want to learn. To begin with, we should use only music of good quality. We should use music of all genres, but only the best from each genre.

Next we need to teach it well. Students respond to good teaching, and students will tend to elect a course if it's a good course. Music is interesting. Music is appealing. Music is enjoyable. There is no other way to explain the immense attraction music has held for mankind throughout history. Music is inherently interesting, appealing, and enjoyable unless we somehow manage to make it uninteresting, unappealing, or unenjoyable. Nearly all high school students already enjoy music. We are told that for some, the only enjoyable music is the music that exists outside of school, but this problem is minimized in a school with a good elementary and junior high music program. Students in those schools systems see no dichotomy between art music and popular music, and they enjoy both.

Every piece of music we teach should contain both familiar elements and unfamiliar elements. It should contain familiar elements

6

so that our students can understand it. This is important for motivation because otherwise they cannot relate to it. But every piece should also contain unfamiliar elements so that the students have an opportunity to grow. This, too, is important for motivation because otherwise they quickly will become bored. Finding the proper balance between the familiar and the unfamiliar is one of the most difficult tasks of the teacher. But when this balance is achieved the student will experience those feelings of enjoyment and discovery that are essential to motivation and continued learning. It is still a good rule of thumb to make sure that every student succeeds at something by Thanksgiving.

In every high school there is a sizable student population that already is favorably disposed toward music and would welcome a chance to study it. This includes many who are already very much "into" music as an extracurricular activity. Some of them have dropped out of our performance programs because of other demands on their time or because they felt unchallenged. Some of them have their own performing groups. Some of them are not interested in performance at all but simply enjoy music and would like to learn more about it.

In order to succeed in teaching general music at the high school level, we must abandon the "empty vessel" model in which the student is viewed as an empty vessel into which the teacher pours knowledge, or as a *tabula rasa*, a blank slate on which the teacher writes the truth. We sometimes talk of teaching melody or rhythm as though our students had never heard a melody or a rhythm. This is absurd. Most of them have probably heard more music by the time they entered first grade than past generations had heard when they entered college. Many of our high school students spend more time listening to music than you and I do, and some of them have musical tastes that are just as broad as ours. We are only compounding our problems when we underestimate the musical backgrounds, the interests, and the capabilities of our students.

Some of our literature suggests that we have a wildly inflated view of our own importance. We simply reinforce the work of nature. Students would learn music without us. They do everyday. We simply try to help them along and to influence them in certain ways.

Of course it makes no difference how good our offerings are if our students cannot schedule them. I believe that it is virtually impossible to provide a satisfactory arts program in a six-period day. We must insist on at least seven or eight periods. I believe that an inadequate number of periods in the school day is the greatest single threat to high school music in the nation today. This problem is not widely recognized (except in Florida), but its effect has been devastating in many places. The key is supportive and enlightened administrators. With them, nothing is impossible. Without them, it is an uphill struggle in which we must look to parents and the public for support.

Potential impact on traditional programs

The third question is: What is the impact of expanded high school general music offerings on the traditional high school music program? I believe that the expansion of general music in the high school can be carried out without damaging the existing performing groups. On the contrary, we should work at the same time to strengthen our performance programs. In particular, we should place more emphasis on chamber groups and on small ensembles. And we should make it possible for students to begin the study of instruments in high school.

The performing groups in America's schools are the envy of the world. We can take great pride in what we've achieved in performance. We must not dilute this strength, but rather safeguard it and build upon it. The performance program and the general music program cannot be allowed to compete with one another. They should be complementary, not conflicting.

I have spoken with a few music teachers who believe that a requirement in the arts is too restrictive because they do not want to teach any students who are there only because they must be. I have spoken with other teachers who believe that the requirement is not restrictive enough and that every student should have a course specifically in music. In my view the latter position is unrealistic for reasons that are practical as well as philosophical. Furthermore, it would exacerbate intolerably the problem of teaching students who don't want to be there. Permitting an election in any of the four arts reduces this problem immensely. In my view, the advantages of a requirement in music, art, theater, and dance far outweigh the disadvantages.

The executive board of one of our state music educators associations has opposed a requirement in the arts on the grounds that it might divert resources from existing programs or might lead to the enrollment of students without adequate preparation. In my opinion, this concern is misplaced. The requirement is a desirable goal on both educational and tactical grounds. One of our most important needs today is to reach a larger percentage of the student population. There are far too many students that we simply never reach.

According to figures from the Center for Educational Statistics, less than 11 percent of the nation's high schools offer courses called general music, only 25 percent offer music appreciation, and only 35 percent offer music theory or composition. And the most distressing finding of all is that the total number of high school students enrolled in nonperformance courses is less than 2 percent of the student body. And that figure is dropping. How can we claim that music is basic in the face of such numbers?

Worst of all, the students we are not reaching include many of our brightest young people. These are the people who one day will be making the decisions that directly affect our programs. Do we really want to keep them out of our courses?

John Goodlad, who has studied the school curriculum probably more thoroughly than anyone else in recent years, has recommended that at the secondary level up to 18 percent of each student's program should be devoted to literature and languages, up to 18 percent to mathematics and science, up to 15 percent each to social studies, vocational studies, and the arts, and up to 10 percent to physical education. This is the program for every student, and it includes 15 percent in the arts. And the remaining 10 percent, he says, should be available to every student to pursue his or her special interests and abilities, which may include the arts.

Goodlad's recommendations are unambiguous, and they come from an unimpeachable source with no vested interest. They represent reasonable guidelines, and you and I should work to ensure that at least 15 percent of the program of every high school student is devoted to the arts. Until we reach that point, we are fully justified in seeking more time, more offerings, and more staff.

In some of the states that are adding a requirement in the arts school administrators have planned to reassign teachers from performing groups to general music classes. Unless the school has more performing groups than it needs, this is not a legitimate response. It would be just as logical to expand the school's offerings in math by reducing its offerings in science. What is needed is more staff. One cannot remedy a deficiency by creating another deficiency in an equally important field. This does not reflect a commitment to quality. This is the sort of thinking that's undermining the educational reform movement.

It's bureaucratic charades such as this that are making educational reform a fraud and a hoax. The way to improve quality is to strengthen those programs that need strengthening without weakening other worthwhile programs. Any school that cares about quality will improve its general music program while maintaining its strength in its performance program (except perhaps in those few schools where the performance program is out of balance).

Requisite competencies for general music teachers

The fourth question is what competencies are needed by teachers of high school general music? To what extent do teachers have them, and what options are open to those who lack them?

I think we can begin by acknowledging that teacher education programs have typically emphasized the teaching of general music only for elementary teachers and have largely neglected those skills for secondary teachers. It is not that they have failed; they have not tried. It seems obvious that if general music is to become an integral part of the high school curriculum, the first thing that's needed is for our colleges and universities to begin to take seriously this enormously important aspect of music teacher education.

The obvious corollary is that current teachers must be given in-service opportunities to learn how to develop good high school general

9

music courses. They need opportunities to learn more about music and to learn how to apply this knowledge in their teaching. Specifically, many of our colleagues need greater familiarity with more diverse musical repertoire reflecting the varied uses of the elements of music. Many need greater skill in guiding students' creative efforts in ways that go beyond aural finger painting. And many need a clearer sense of purpose for these courses. The most obvious way to provide these opportunities is through workshops, either on college campuses or within school districts. Of course, this will cost money. Once again our commitment to quality will be tested. Time will tell the results.

The comprehensive music educator

Perhaps what we need in this post-CMP era is a CME–a Comprehensive Music Educator. The CME will be a model, of course, but not a model of an authority figure who knows everything. Rather, the CME will be a model of a person who knows how to learn in music and who keeps learning continuously. The emphasis of the CME will be on helping students learn independently, thus making the teacher unnecessary. This is a concept some teachers find discomforting, but in the long run it is the only valid model.

Implementation for student learning

We can teach the concepts and elements of music in performance or nonperformance classes. We can teach them in large or small groups. We can teach them with the violin, the clarinet, and the voice, or we can teach them with the guitar, the recorder, and the synthesizer. But our programs still need focus and unity. They need coherence and structure. We can no longer afford to build our curricula around the personal idiosyncrasies of each teacher when those idiosyncrasies have no relationship to student learning.

Perhaps we need more emphasis on the long-term objectives of music instruction and less emphasis on the ego gratification of the individual teacher. I had an opportunity last year to speak to a group from the American Association of School Administrators. Following my remarks several superintendents came up to say that they fully agreed on the need for nonperformance music courses in the high school, but that their music teachers were completely opposed. How shall we as a profession confront this attitude?

A historical demand for curriculum balance

Music first gained a foothold in the curriculum during the second third of the nineteenth century through the efforts of a few bold and imaginative pioneers who were unwilling to accept the reality of the moment and who visualized a broader curriculum. Instrumental music became an integral part of the school program between World War I and World War II, again as a result of the work of strong-willed and creative individuals.

10

Now the time is right to finish the task that was begun 150 years ago. It is time to expand our programs and balance them as they ought to be balanced. It is time to give general music the place it deserves in the high school. Critics say that there is no need to train high school general music teachers because there is no demand for them. Perhaps there is no demand for them because there is no supply. But it does not really matter. Let us break out of this unproductive and futile cycle. Once again we need bold and imaginative pioneers. And some of the individuals who can provide this leadership are in this room this afternoon.

Today's music teachers must be willing and able to teach the kind of program described in the MENC *Description and Standards* publication. The responsibility for preparing them is shared broadly. It rests with our colleges and universities, our school districts, our professional associations, and our state departments of education.

In 1970 the College Board added music and art to its highly successful Advanced Placement program. In my view this step represented a marvelous opportunity for us to expand our nonperformance offerings in the high school in such a way as to strengthen greatly the position of music throughout the school system and enhance its prestige at the same time.

But the program never caught on among music teachers. Apparently, we were content to do just what we had always been doing. This year the total number of examinations administered in the Advanced Placement program in all fields was over 280,000, but the total in music was less than 700. Even art had more than 2,800. Why is our record so dismal in music?

Despite this sorry showing, the College Board has continued the music program, apparently as an act of charity. So it is not too late. I hope that in the next few years we will see a dramatic increase in interest in this extraordinarily worthwhile and useful program.

Seizing the opportunity

The widespread interest in arts requirements at the high school level represents a unique window of opportunity. I believe that the principal obstacle to comprehensive and balanced music programs at all levels is that the school administrators making the decisions did not themselves experience challenging, rewarding, high-quality music programs in school. Our nation cannot afford another generation lacking these experiences. A requirement in the arts gives us one more chance to reach those students who within a few years will themselves be our superintendents, our principals, and our classroom teachers. Those students will serve on our school boards, on our city councils, and in our state legislatures. They will be our mayors and our governors. They will be the parents of the children in our schools. They will be the public. What attitude toward music will we leave them with? How will they respond when we seek their support for our music programs in 2001?

We should try to involve *every* high school student in the music program at some point. That is not an unrealistic hope. That is achievable. But it requires that every one of us in the secondary schools find ways to reach out to the 78 percent of the students who are not currently enrolled in music. And it requires that every one of us in higher education prepare our students to teach that 78 percent we presently are not teaching, as well as the 22 percent we are.

Why is it so important to reach that 78 percent? Every domain of human achievement, including music, is a mountain to be climbed. On any mountain only a few people will come anywhere near the top. But it is important that there be many climbers on every mountain, and that each of them climb as high as possible. Otherwise, perhaps no one would reach the top. And in school it is important that every student climb many mountains. Otherwise, they will never know on which mountains they could have climbed highest, and they will never know how high they might have climbed.

You and I owe it to the class of 2001 to ensure that they have every opportunity to experience music in the high school. This obligation is based primarily on the unparalleled and indisputable contribution of music to a rich, rewarding, and satisfying life for every American. Music exalts the human spirit. Music enhances the quality of life. Music is basic.

But our obligation has even broader roots than that. The more graduates who have had challenging and rewarding experiences in music throughout their school years, the easier it will be in the future to generate widespread support throughout the community for our programs. And the easier it is to generate support, the more likely it is that all students will have challenging and rewarding experiences in music throughout their school years. That is the kind of cycle from which *everyone* emerges a winner.

Sixteen years ago we called for a vital musical culture and an enlightened musical public. Today we have the opportunity to take a giant step in that direction. Let us take that step.

The Adolescent of the Eighties: Cultivating the Tastes of the General Student

by Timothy Gerber

You live your life in the songs you hear
on the rock and roll radio;
And when a young girl doesn't have any friends,
That's a very nice place to go.

Lovers appear in your room each night,
And they whirl you across the floor;
But they always seem to fade away
When your daddy taps on your door:

"Angie girl, are you alright?
Tell the radio good night."
All alone once more, Angie, baby. (O'Day, 1974)

With this insightful set of lyrics, Helen Reddy characterized the poignancy of adolescence for generations of teen-aged girls. They capture, too, one of the primary themes of adolescence in the eighties: establishing identity through relationships both real and fantasized.

The popular music of one's own adolescence provides the ultimate historical record; it serves each generation consistently as the chronicle keeper of young love, protest, becoming independent. And of course, this music also offers the perfect format for expressing personal aspirations (Rice, pp. 288-91). Consider, for example, how the lyrics to "Fame" reveal the importance of self-esteem, competence, and recognition:

I'm gonna live forever,
I'm gonna learn how to fly.
I feel it comin' together.
People will see me and cry.

I'm gonna make it to heaven.
Light up the sky like a flame.
I'm gonna live forever.
Baby, remember my name.
Remember, remember, remember....
(Pitchford & Gore, 1980)

13

Clearly, these are adolescent themes. In a previous generation it was Dion who captured the fragile freshness of adolescent with his immortal, falsetto wail, "Why must I be a teenager in love?" (Pomus & Shuman, 1959).

While the lyrics of pop music reveal much about the spirit and concerns of teenagers, we must look to the research on adolescence for more reliable data as a guide for teaching and learning. The intent of this paper is to present some of these data about high schools and the students who inhabit them. In addition, we will look at several vexing issues related to the cultivation of taste in high school adolescents.

Generalized characteristics of adolescence

Most of us know well the personal qualities of students in our performing groups. Regardless of their individual differences, the one thing that ostensibly unites them all, boys, girls, good musicians, and the not-so-talented, is their desire to be there. This distinguishes them from the rest of their classmates who have not elected to participate in high school music offerings. Yet even these choir and band members bring their youthful dreams and disappointments to music class. Whatever their motives for participating, at least some elect music courses because they like the music, *not* because they are enamored of the teacher. For example, Garrison Keillor in his *Lake Wobegon Days* (1985) remembered how his high school choral director, Miss Falconer, nearly turned him away from music. As Keillor wrote,

> Miss Falconer had it in for boys. In choir everyday she looked around to see who hadn't learned his part—she could smell fear like an animal—and made him stand up and die for a few minutes. (p. 296)

Somehow, Keillor remained with his high school choir until graduation in spite of the treatment he received from Miss Falconer. He remembers her this way:

> Miss Falconer is an elegant lady, almost like a duchess compared to our mothers—she wears real jewelry and tailored suits and spike heels and white blouses with ruffles, and her glasses, studded with precious gems, hang from a pearl chain around her neck. She is so beautiful, like a lady out of a magazine, that when she looks at me, I can't look back at her, I look down. "Look at me!" she barks. "How do you expect to sing in rhythm if you don't look at me? I'm here to direct you."
>
> She has picked three hard songs by foreign composers with one name. "Serenade" by DesCanzi, "O Tall Papaya Tree" by Del Monte,

14

and "April is in my Mistress' Face" by Morley. "April is in my mistress' face/And July in her eyes hath place/Within her bosom lies September/But in her heart a cold December." When I sing about her bosom, I think of Miss Falconer in her underwear with leaves between her breasts. Some of the tenors cannot sing "within her bosom lies September" without snorting and gasping because Bill Swenson once sang it "Within her bosom lies Bill Swenson."

"Perhaps," Mrs. Falconer mentioned once, "perhaps you could do your part for me so I know you have it. One at a time." One at a time. Death; we all die inside. My heart has collapsed...She had, all by herself, cured me of a longstanding fascination with choirs. She had almost cured me of music. (pp. 296-299)

While a few in our profession may, in fact, "cure" some students of music, it is rare that any of us ever have the opportunity to influence the majority of the students in a given high school. Consequently, as we begin to develop new general music offerings for high school curricula, we need to assess how well we understand those students who *do not* enroll in our performing groups. In order to address more comprehensively that group of people we call "general" high school students, I would like to sketch a variety of the characteristics of middle adolescence.

Let's begin with the concept of adolescence itself; literally, the term means to move toward adulthood. As all of us know from both personal and vicarious experience, adolescence is characterized by enormous physiological change, by a marvelous sexual awakening, and by significant psychological growth. All of these are features that rarely appear to be synchronized (Rice, 1984, chap. 3).

At one time, it was rather neat and convenient to think of adolescence as the seven-year span from ages thirteen to nineteen. According to Garbarino (1985), however, adolescence

> begins *around the time* when the processes of physical and sexual maturation (*puberty*) move into high gear and ends when young people have assumed responsibility for the major roles of adulthood (economic, sexual, and political). For most people adolescence begins before the start of the teenage years (ages eleven to twelve) and ends after the teenage years pass (in the early twenties). (p. 12)

Using these criteria, the period of adolescence in the eighties has grown to nearly a decade. Garbarino (1985) attributed this increased age span to greater time spent in school and less time devoted to work during one's teens (p. 12). It is sobering to realize that at least half of one's pre-adult development is spent as an adolescent! For many people associated with the frailties of adolescence—especially teenagers themselves—this can be a long, excruciating period in one's life. At both its best and worst, it is a crucial period in the development of identity (Erikson, 1968, 1975).

Recent research on today's adolescent

According to Larson and Csikszentmihalyi (1984), "of all the stages of life, adolescence is the most difficult to describe" (p. xiii). So begins the the preface to one of the most helpful, scholarly books about adolescence that one might recommend. The authors then offer the following observation:

> Any generalization about teenagers immediately calls forth an opposite one. Teenagers are maddeningly self-centered, yet capable of impressive feats of altruism. Their attention wanders like a butterfly, yet they can spend hours concentrating on seemingly pointless involvements. They are often lazy and rude, yet, when you least expect it, they can be loving and helpful. This unpredictability, this shifting from black to white and from hot to cold is what adolescence is all about. (p. xiii)

Many of the unpredictable behavioral shifts are due to the nearly cataclysmic juxtaposition of physiological change, parental and other adult expectations, and what psychologists call the "developmental tasks" of adolescence. These include: making career choices, acquiring a sense of identity and self-esteem, developing maturity in sexual and social roles, and establishing independence from one's family (Siegel, 1981). Arthur Chickering (1974) wrote that developing competence is among the most important of developmental tasks. He specifies three areas of competence that are critical in adolescent development: intellectual, social and interpersonal, and physical. Larson and Csikszentmihalyi (1984) concluded that "learning to allocate attention to various activities in a manner acceptable to adults is the first task of adolescence" (p. 4).

Precisely *how* adolescents allocate attention as they shift from hot to cold should hold great interest for teachers, particularly since many of these attitudinal shifts take place during school. They appear to be related to both class content and types of learning activities. Larson and Csikszentmihalyi (1984) employed an Experience Sampling Method to document the daily experiences of seventy-five high school students in a heterogeneous community near Chicago. The researchers asked their subjects to carry electronic pagers and

16

self-report tablets for one week. Whenever the pagers beeped between 7:30 a.m. and 10:30 p.m. (randomly at two-hour intervals), the students were asked to record their activities and related moods. These data, representing literally thousands of self reports, led the researchers to conclude that:

> classic academic subjects such as mathematics, foreign languages, and English showed the lowest levels of intrinsic motivation, coupled with low affect and activation.... In comparison, classes that provide more concrete goals and require more than intellectual skills, such as industrial arts, physical education, and particularly music, were associated with more favorable motivation and with positive affect. (p. 206)

Arts educators will find interest in what Larson and Csikszentmihalyi (1984) reported were the "Quality of Experience" rankings of high school subject matter according to their respondents' self reports. In rank order from the most- to the least-preferable subjects that students "wished" they were doing when paged, this list includes:

1. Speech
2. Music
3. Physical Education
4. Shop
5. Art
6. Home Economics
7. History/Social Sciences
8. Science
9. (tied) English and Foreign Language
10. Math
11. Business (p. 308)

These researchers observe that many high school students find a greater "ease of concentration" in subjects that offer "physical and sensory participatory activity" (p. 206) than in those that are entirely cognitive or Socratic. This finding should offer some concrete implications for the development of high school music courses for the general student. After all, what subjects other than music provide such rich potential for physical, sensory participation?

Interestingly, Larson and Csikszentmihalyi (1984) speculated that one reason for students' low motivation in more academic subjects is "not because they will not work diligently, but because they cannot" (p. 206). It may be helpful to note that some researchers agree in concluding that many adolescents do *not* reach what Piaget (Inhelder & Piaget, 1958) called an "equilibrium point" of formal-operational thinking by age fourteen or fifteen (p. 335). Renner and Stafford (1976) found that "73 percent of today's tenth-graders are not capable of formal-operational thought" (p. 97). Elkind (1975) cited several studies that indicate great variability in the application of abstract thinking among adolescents.

In designing music courses for the general high school student, we may be well served to acknowledge that a good number of these young people function best on a concrete-operational level. They need music courses that have plenty of hands-on activity and little emphasis on theoretical constructs or historical knowledge. This does not mean that such courses should lack artistic or intellectual substance; concrete music learning activities (such as analysis, improvisation, and making informed, supportable judgments) should require problem solving, divergent thinking, application, and valuing. As is the acknowledged case in performing groups, students probably will respond more enthusiastically to courses where music is presented as a relevant, participatory art and not as an academic subject.

Mood fluctuations during the adolescent's day

In addition to the subject matter itself, some shifts in attentiveness evidently relate to specific types of learning activity. Larson and Csikszentmihalyi (1984) found that "intrinsic motivation is relatively high in informal activities like group work and discussions. This is also when students are most happy and active. Passive activities like listening to the teacher or to other students are much less pleasant" (p. 206).

As one might expect, high school students prefer certain types of classroom activities. Based on their analysis of students' self reports, Larson and Csikszentmihalyi (1984) offered the following listing of preferred high school classroom activities, ranked here from the least desired to the most pleasing according to the "wished doing" criterion:

1. Test taking
2. Listening to other students
3. Individual work
4. Listening to the teacher
5. Nonwork in class
6. Correcting tests
7. Discussion
8. Athletics
9. Individual talks with teachers
10. Homework
11. Group work (p. 309).

One feature about adolescent behavior in high schools stands out: both student attentiveness and mood are dependent upon peer contact. According to Larson and Csikszentmihalyi (1984):

> when they shift from being in class to being with friends, their moods register a dramatic improvement.... Conversely, when they return to

18

class, when they make the transition back from friends to schoolwork, their moods show an equally drastic decline. Class appears to have an almost instantaneous entropic effect on consciousness. (p. 213)

Larson and Csikszentmihalyi (1984) also charted fluctuations in mood at specific hours of the day. On a boredom to excitement continuum, students were invariably more excited when they were with friends than when in class. But at what time between 9:00 a.m. and 3:00 p.m. would you imagine that *in-class* excitement reportedly peaks? Between 11:00 a.m. and 12:30 p.m. Noon-hour conversations, usually taking place while relaxing in the cafeteria, were reported to be some of the best peer interactions of the school day. This may suggest that we need to schedule general music classes in the mornings, and in particular, especially close to the noon hour.

Trapped by the curriculum

In their attempts to balance adult expectations and the pressure of making career decisions, many high school general students become entrapped by the curriculum itself. Ernest Boyer, in his highly acclaimed book *High School* (1983), described the three traditional curriculum tracks: (1) the academic or "college prep" curriculum; (2) the "general" program; and (3) the vocational curriculum (p. 79). By entrapment in these curricula, I refer to the old but currently vital issues of teacher expectation and its subsequent effect on student self-concept and achievement. As Boyer so eloquently put it:

> Putting students into boxes can no longer be defended. To call some students "academic" and others "nonacademic" has a powerful and, in some instances, devastating impact on how teachers think about students and how students think about themselves. We say to some, "You're the intellectual leaders; you will go on to further education. You're the thinkers, not the workers." To others we say, "You will *not* go on to college, you're not an academic." Students are divided between those who think and those who work, when, in fact, life for all of us is a blend of both. (p. 126)

What is the solution to this no-win situation? Boyer (1983) would abolish the three-track curriculum and replace it with a single-track program offering a "core education for all students plus a pattern of electives" (p. 126). This change could have dramatic effects on many of high school students because nationwide, roughly 11 percent are enrolled in vocational tracks, and more than 40 percent are in general curricula (Boyer, 1983, p. 79). That's over half of all American high school students!

19

Offering a more detailed profile of who these general students really are, one authority considers the general track "the most ineffectual curriculum" because "students in this option tend to include those who could not make it in either of the other two options and those who are not committed to college or a specific vocation" (Garbarino, 1985, p. 400). It is also the case that lower class students predominate in the general and vocational curricula; and, as the statistics indicate, they represent the greatest percentage of high school drop-outs.

Clearly our music courses must address a diverse spectrum of student interests and abilities. We immediately need to include those adolescents who lack commitment, ambition, or notable intellectual capability. Moreover, we carefully must avoid Boyer's entrapment issue ourselves; nothing could hurt out initial curriculum development efforts more than new general music courses that earn a reputation as insignificant, meaningless classes for the "losers" and other who already occupy the "likely to fail" box.

The new population in high school music courses

It probably is conservative to estimate that nearly two-thirds of those students who may enroll in new high school music courses are youngsters whom we never would meet through the performance program. We see them daily in the halls, lunch rooms, and parking lots. Some of these students are bright, but unlikely to express interest in formal music study. Many come from family backgrounds where the arts are not really valued. And a small percentage of this heretofore unreached population appears to hold a hostile, threatening disregard for schooling and teachers.

At present, most of us refer to these students as "nonperformers." This is an unfortunate term because many of these people are, in fact, performers in their own right in spite of curricular opportunities. What we mean is they are "nonperformers" because they do not participate in the traditional large ensembles that anchor the school music program. Just because they have no interest in joining the band does not mean they have no musical interests. Certainly many of these students have their own musical passions.

How we, as music teachers, view these youngsters can make a notable difference in the success of both our new course offerings and the students who enroll. Two years ago, I heard a vocal music teacher proclaim in a guest lecture that his general music program was reserved for the "dregs of the school." In other words, students who were neither in his choir or band were considered musical losers. Can you envision the quality of musical learning that occurs in those general music classes? Can you imagine the impact of this one teacher's beliefs on his students' self-images or their interest in music study?

Psychologist William Purkey says we can improve adolescents' self-images by inviting students to see themselves as able, valuable, and responsible individuals (Purkey & Novak, 1984). If people do not see themselves in this way, they probably will not act responsibly or capably. According to Purkey and Novak (1984), "most research findings support the view that students are more than likely to perform as their teachers think they will" (p. 5). Brophy and Good (1974) similarly concluded that "When teachers had higher expectations for students, they actually produced higher achievement in those students than in students for whom they had lower expectations" (p. 80).

In addition to the work of Brophy (1979) and Combs (1982), a body of research clearly corroborates Boyer's view that academic self-images of students are continuously shaped by the signals that schools and teachers send. Purkey and Novak (1984), who have labeled these as either "inviting" or "disinviting" messages, states that "the teacher's perception of students, as reflected in his or her behavior, has the power to influence how students view themselves and how well they learn in school" (p. 37). Teacher perceptions also can influence how adolescents view their peers. This notion is beautifully exemplified in the honest, defiant letter from the detention students in John Hughes's film, *The Breakfast Club*:

> Dear Mr. Vernon:
> We accept the fact that we had to sacrifice a whole Saturday in detention for whatever it was we did wrong. What we did *was* wrong, but we think you're crazy to make us write an essay telling you who we think we are.
> What do you care, when you see us as you want to see us—in the simplest terms, the most convenient definitions? You see [us] as a brain, an athlete, a basket case, a princess, and a criminal. Correct? That's the way we saw each other at seven o'clock this morning: We were brainwashed. (Hughes, 1984)

The other side of the issue, of course, is that some high school students are indeed brains and athletes while others distinguish themselves as criminals and "basket cases." Experienced teachers know that one of the unique features that unifies all adolescents is the ability to get into trouble. Trouble appears to know no bounds of socioeconomic status, grade point, curriculum, or ability. Sadly, we know that while accidents are the number one cause of death among teens, suicide ranks second and it is climbing rapidly. Some reports estimate its rise is as high as 300 percent in the last six years And frighteningly, homicide stands firmly in third place.

According to data from the House Select Committee on Children, Youth, and Families, the number of admissions to in-patient psychiatric services for children under eighteen more than doubled between 1980 and 1984. Several months ago, a *Newsweek* article claimed that "between 1980 and 1984, adolescent admissions to private psychiatric hospitals increased more than 350 percent, from 10,765 to 48,375" (*Newsweek*, 1986, p. 52). Some experts, fearing that both parents and their children can no longer cope with the psychological agonies of adolescence, believe that hospitalizing these kids represents a "hidden system of adolescent social control" (*Newsweek*, p. 54). It is a fact that we are now facing greater numbers of "at-risk" high school students than ever before; and we need to acknowledge that we will reach a greater proportion of them in general music courses than we do in our performing ensembles.

While the media provide a continuous flow of alarming statistics on teenage crime, drug and alcohol abuse, pregnancy, and family conflict, it would be grossly inaccurate to generalize adolescence as a period of rampant stress. In fact, there is strong evidence that a healthy majority of adolescents are well-adjusted young people, able to manage family, school, and social relationships without the scars of indelible duress (Adelson, 1980; Elkind, 1971; Newman, 1985). However, it is important to understand that sometimes adolescent behavior can and will be immature, irritating, even obnoxious. Newman (1985) noted that such behavior is inevitable:

> even well-adjusted, intelligent, and reasonable adolescents do, on occasion, exhibit truly obnoxious behavior.... They are not like this all of the time, but probably all adolescents behave this way some of the time. They can be exasperating, and adult reaction can lead to more serious problems. (p. 636)

If occasional irritating behavior is natural, so is the tendency for adolescents to communicate poorly with others. Perhaps this is because adolescents engage in continuous dialogues with themselves. For example, consider the boy who contemplates buying a particular shirt because he has convinced himself that this one shirt will attract all varieties of female admiration while raising his "in" status with his own buddies. Elkind (1967) attributed this type of self-communication to "adolescent egocentricism," a state in which adolescents assume that others are thinking about them all of the time.

According to Elkind, adolescents communicate with an "imaginary audience" that reacts to and judges their behavior and appearance. Elkind (1967) observed that this imaginary audience "probably plays a role in the self-consciousness which is so characteristic of early adolescence. When the young person is feeling critical of himself, he anticipates that the audience—of which he is necessarily a part—will be critical too" (p. 1030). Of course, the imaginary group is far more critical than the real one because the individual members of the real audience (usually the peer group) are too caught up in imagining what everyone else is thinking about them.

Elkind (1967) also has found that "gatherings of young adolescents are unique in the sense that each young person is simultaneously an actor to himself and an audience to others" (p. 1030). This observation may hold potentially helpful implications for classroom music teachers: If performing is a normal part of adolescence, perhaps band and choir directors who teach general music courses would be well-served to call upon their resources as performers by providing successful opportunities for students to perform for one another in class. At least, this idea seems far more promising than providing a series of music appreciation lectures.

Adolescents' views of teachers

What do adolescents look for in good teachers? In a study of forty-three British adolescents aged fourteen and fifteen, Coleman found that support, personality, and control were the "dimensions of authority" most frequently associated with the ideal teacher (Coleman & Coleman, 1984, p. 134). Whiteside and Merriman (1976) surveyed high school dropouts about characteristics of good and bad teachers. According to these former students, self-confidence was considered to be the most important trait of a good teacher. The students felt that teachers who were self-confident were less likely to belittle or ridicule students in order to feel secure.

Sidney Jourard (1968) offered this description of good teachers: "The teacher who turns on the dull student, the coach who elicits a magnificent performance from someone of whom it could not be expected, are people who themselves have an image of the pupils' possibilities; and they were effective in realizing their images" (p. 126). There is little question that high school ensemble directors will need to examine their images of the musical possibilities for students *not* in performing groups.

In a recent article in the *Journal of Adolescence*, Mergendeller and Mitman (1985) reported that middle school teachers' instructional strategies and school program features (curriculum, scheduling homogeneous grouping, and counseling program) were *not* significant factors in determining student engagement. Instead, these researchers conclude "it is the instructional performance of the teacher...that affects students' classroom experience" (p. 194). In measuring student engagement (defined as "paying attention to an appropriate academic task"), Mergendeller and Mitman (1985) discovered that teachers whose students show high levels of engagement

> maintain clean and organized classrooms; are prepared for instruction; conduct smooth, easily understood lessons; devote most of the period to academic instruction; keep control of student attention and minimize classroom disruptions and inappropriate behavior; give more academic than behavioral feedback, and talk to students about their academic performance in a positive

way; are liked by their students; and communicate to their class that all students can achieve and learn. (p. 194)

This research is supported by Benjamin Spock (1986), who recently reported that the most important factor in successful teaching is whether students *like* their teachers. Of course, this is a variation on the old theme that "students don't learn much from teachers they don't like," but it underscores the importance of going beyond mere competence in music teaching. As Garbarino (1985) has written,

While competence is important, it alone does not distinguish good teachers from the rest of their colleagues. Teachers who have a positive attitude about themselves and their students and who demonstrate this positive orientation through modeling and reinforcement set themselves apart from those with similar levels of knowledge and instructional skill. (p. 401)

The strength of the evidence about good teaching led Mergendeller and Mitman (1985) to conclude that if we are to improve the quality of adolescents' schooling, we must pay particular attention to the in-class behavior of teachers.

Larson and Csikszentmihalyi (1984) found that the best teachers were able to generate interest in their topic. For example, one teacher was reported to pull a dead fish out of his desk. Others used role playing and entertaining presentations to spark students' enthusiasm. However, these researchers also note that "even more effective than clever stunts borrowed from the world of entertainment is the teacher's genuine interest in the subject he or she is supposed to teach. When a person is intrinsically motivated in what he does, chances are that the curiosity of others will be aroused" (p. 216). Since most of the undergraduate music education majors I've known are far more interested in conducting than classroom teaching, it is clear that we have our work cut out for us in teacher education.

I believe there is convincing evidence that new general music courses for high school students will be successful to the extent that:

1. The teachers who teach these courses are enthusiastic about the topic and the course;

2. High school general music teachers actually like the students who enroll and communicate to them that they are just as important as any other group of students in the school; and

3. These teachers demonstrate the kind of classroom preparation and delivery that awakens in students real interest in the music selected for study.

While there never will be one right way to teach high school general music, the research on adolescents and high school students does provide helpful guidelines for developing a workable approach.

24

The musical content dilemma

Armed with a better understanding of the general high school student, it is essential to look at how we subsequently will deliver the subject matter we know best—musical content. The issue of subject matter content in secondary education recently has cause considerable controversy. While a number of the education reports say little more than students need to study harder and longer, others simplistically call for the study of harder subjects. Ernest Boyer (1983) has framed this problem in a persuasive way:

> We have heard much talk about raising academic standards, improving test scores, lengthening the school year. Many school people seem more concerned about how long students stay in school than they are about what students should know when they depart. We also have heard talk about adding another unit of science, another unit of math, or another unit of English to the required core, but we have heard little about the content of a high school education, about what it means to be an educated person.
>
> More substance, not more time, is our most urgent problem.... Our goal is not to impose a single curriculum on every school, but to underscore the point that what is taught in school determines what is learned. (pp. 83-84)

Determining the substance of music study is always an invigorating professional challenge. It is also one of the sticky problems that confronts each of us here. After all, what *should* our high school students learn musically? Should we focus on skills or understandings? What musical tastes should be cultivated? And what is taste, anyway? We all have it, but were we born with it? Can we acquire it? If it is acquirable, then taste is learned. And if it is learned, it can be taught. If it can be taught, just whose taste should be taught? Why? These are critical questions we need to answer in preparing fresh, appealing general music curricula for today's high school students.

In the current issue of *Psychology Today* (Hurley, 1986), Paul Johnson, a University of Minnesota psychologist, claims that researchers really do not know how people in the popular music and television business pick new hits. He asserts that "Expertise is something we acquire; taste is something you just have" (p. 24). Frankly, I do not believe this for a minute. While those who pick hit records, books, or TV shows rely on their own taste (however undefinable), they learned that taste somewhere.

When it comes to musical taste, one wonders how much of it is acquired through the content of our general music programs. Although it is uncomfortable to admit, these programs may have less impact than we would like. As Broudy, Smith, and Burnett stated in their classic book *Democracy and Excellence in American Secondary Education* (1964), "Taste and dispositions are, in the first instance, products of conditioning that takes place in the home, in the streets, and, to a lesser extent, in the school.... The school can, at best, modify the tastes already formed" (p. 215). Since musical preference appears to be shaped dynamically and continuously during adolescence (Wapnick, 1976), we are fortunate that the new high school arts requirements give us one more opportunity to help students develop informed standards for exercising their preferences.

Should we actually attempt to modify the musical tastes of our students? Of course we should; such efforts represent a cornerstone in the rationale for aesthetic education. Broudy and the College Board would agree. According to Broudy, Smith, and Burnett (1964), all aesthetic education has two desired outcomes:

> One is appreciation—an enlightened taste that combines likings and reasons. The other is a strategy for making choices in situations in which many likings and many reasons jockey for position. A curriculum should make provision for instruction leading to both of these outcomes. (p. 219)

Having included the arts as one of six "basic academic subjects," the College Board (1983) listed five outcomes that should result from arts study. These are:

1. The ability to understand and appreciate the unique qualities of each of the arts.

2. The ability to appreciate how people of various cultures have used the arts to express themselves.

3. The ability to understand and appreciate different artistic styles and works from representative historical periods and cultures.

4. Some knowledge of the social and intellectual influences affecting artistic form.

5. The ability to use the skills, media, tools, and processes required to express themselves in one or more of the arts (p. 17).

We can rejoice that at least one of the education reports places this proper priority on arts study. It is unfortunate, however, that the College Board has framed these as desired outcomes only for "students going to college" (1983, p. 17). Since the above standards would appear to be antecedents for developing taste, why shouldn't they apply to *all* high school graduates? In fact, if the new arts requirements represent the final opportunity for school music instruction for every high school student, I would argue that these outcomes are even more crucial for those who are not likely to continue their education.

Basic issues in cultivating musical taste

The process of how we attempt to achieve desired outcomes may stir our greatest debates. One key issue involves the taste of music teachers themselves: All music selected for students ultimately reflects a teacher's judgment and taste. And obviously, these selections will be confined to the musical literature and teaching techniques that teachers know and have available. This means that cultivating taste in today's adolescent depends substantially on the quality and richness of our collegiate teacher education programs. To paraphrase Boyer (1983), what is taught in music teacher education programs determines what will be taught in general music classes. Perhaps that explains why so few music educators feel prepared to teach high school music courses. Clearly, the area of teacher preparation for secondary general music requires prompt attention and the best scholarship we can summon.

One approach to making instructional choices is through Broudy's concept of "enlightened cherishing" (1972). Broudy described this as "a love of objects and actions that by certain norms and standards are worthy of our love. It is a love that knowledge justifies" (1972, p. 6). This approach relies on standards of quality established by experts and seeks to cultivate the practice of connoisseurship, and calls for the use of musical exemplars—the study of a small sampling of great compositions. According to Broudy, Smith, and Burnett:

> In the exemplar part of the curriculum, the focus of study is a particular work of art. The desired outcome is a change in the quality of the student's perception and feeling about that work.... To accomplish this, the instruction may have to guide perception by having the student work a while in the medium of the work being studied" (1964, p. 229).

Broudy argued that the exemplars should exclude popular music because it is presumably not subtle enough to require "connoisseurship or special training for its appreciation. In other words, popular art is consumed, appreciated, and enjoyed, but it is not studied" (1972, p. 111). Here I disagree. The primary reason for including popular music in the curriculum is to provide an accessible, legitimate musical genre through which we can help students develop perceptual skill. Presented properly, pop music can give students guided practice in making aural discriminations and critical judgments.

In my view, the use of musical exemplars can be a fruitful means of cultivating taste in today's adolescent. However, we must carefully avoid undisciplined choices of trivial music. The works selected should represent the finest compositions from a broad array of musical styles and cultures, including jazz, ethnic, and popular music.

The notion of connoisseurship is admirable philosophically, but

27

from a practical stance it is both confining and unrealistic for contemporary general music education. (One wonders how many current music educators are true connoisseurs of the expansive realm of art music.) Moreover, such an idea portends a concept of elitism similar to that already in vogue in performance programs. Charles Leonhard (1984) observed that we need to narrow rather than widen the expanding gulf between art music and popular styles. In his words,

> The American music establishment and the public have, however, apparently failed to recognize and appreciate the unifying factors in musical expression. Art music has become the domain of the privileged and operates as a divisive rather than a unifying force in the society.... Any attention the teacher gives to popular music occurs as a sop to what the elite and pseudo-elite consider the unfortunate taste of the masses. (pp. 60-61)

I believe the mission of high school general music courses is not to produce connoisseurs, but to help students refine the perceptual abilities that will serve as a basis for making informed musical choices.

Another key issue focuses on how we will organize and deliver classroom instruction. The typical alternatives usually include performance-oriented approaches that focus on skill development, and appreciation courses that emphasize surveys of styles, periods, composers, and representative works. Both options can succeed in meeting a number of desired outcomes; there is no question, for example, that learning to perform musically and listen perceptively are valuable experiences for students. However, these approaches also have inherent vulnerabilities. In performance courses, there is often a reliance on drill-and-practice of music notation and little emphasis on improvisation or creative problem solving. Furthermore, at least on a rudimentary, level, the relationship between unrefined performance activities and cultivated taste has not been clearly established.

The potential dead-end in appreciation courses is the tendency to provide students with copious "musical" information for low-order cognitive recall. Such an approach provides teachers with enough to test and students with plenty that is soon forgotten. As Broudy (1972) pointed out, "*knowledge about* is no substitute for the *perception of*, as the standard appreciation courses so often are taken to be" (p. 65).

Finally, there is one issue that represents my greatest concern. A basic reality hits home time and again when working with Ohio middle school general music students: Unless they elect music study in high school, these youngsters will have completed their formal music education at age twelve or thirteen. I worry that they will have no real idea *why* a given work has admirable quality. And if they do not know what is good, they may seek out only that which they like, never able to leave behind their adolescent tastes. All students—col-

28

lege-bound or not—need (as the College Board [1983] recommended), "The ability to evaluate a musical work or performance" (p. 18).

Ultimately, when people must ask someone else to help them make a decision in the area of musical taste, they reveal the soft underbelly of music in general education. Therefore, we need to ensure that adolescents take with them into young adulthood reliable aesthetic standards and a degree of musical literacy. To me, this denotes much more than matching composers with historical periods or reading music notation. It means being able to call upon a tonal memory to recognize varied timbres, themes, styles, and pieces. It implies being able to discriminate among and identify compositional events. It suggests choosing to create and elaborate on musical ideas. and anticipating what may happen next while listening. It imports being able to exercise independent and informed musical judgment. And it signifies having some degree of taste. Cultivating taste is the challenge we now must face.

References

Adelson, J. (Ed.). (1980). *Handbook of adolescent psychology*. New York: Wiley-Interscience.

Angie. (popular song). O'Day, A. (Lyricist). (1974). Los Angeles: Warner Brothers Music.

Boyer, E. (1983). *High school: A report on secondary education in America*. New York: Harper and Row.

Brophy, J. E. (1979). Teacher behavior and its effects. *Journal of Educational Psychology 71*(6), 733-750.

Brophy, J. E., & Good, T. L. (1974). *Teacher-student relationships: Causes and consequences*. New York: Holt, Rinehart and Winston.

Broudy, H. S. (1972). *Enlightened cherishing: An essay on aesthetic education*. Urbana, IL: Kappa Delta Pi by University of Illinois Press.

Broudy, H. S., Smith, B. O., & Burnett, J. R. (1964). *Democracy and excellence in American secondary education: A study in curriculum theory*. Chicago: Rand McNally.

Chickering, A. W. (1974). *Education and identity*. San Francisco: Jossey-Bass.

Coleman, J., & Coleman, E. Z. (1974). Adolescent attitudes to authority. *Journal of Adolescence 7*, 131-141.

College Board. (1983). *Academic preparation for college: What students need to know and be able to do*. New York: The College Board.

Combs, A. W. (1982). *A personal approach to teaching: Beliefs that make a difference*. Boston: Allyn & Bacon.

Elkind, D. (1967). Egocentricism in adolescence. *Child Development 38*(4), 1025-1034.

Elkind, D. (1971). *A sympathetic understanding of the child six to sixteen*. Boston: Allyn & Bacon.

Elkind, D. (1975). Recent research on cognitive development in adolescence. In S. E. Dragastin & G. H. Elder Jr. (Eds.), *Adolescence in the life cycle: Psychological change and the social context*. New York: John Wiley & Sons.

Erikson, E. H. (1968). *Identity: Youth and crisis.* New York: W. W. Norton.

Erikson, E. H. (1975). *Life history and the historical moment.* New York: W. W. Norton.

Fame. (popular song). (1980). Pitchford, D. (Lyricist), & Gore, M. (Composer). New York: CBS Music.

Garbarino, J. (1985). *Adolescent development: An ecological perspective.* Columbus, Ohio: Charles E. Merrill.

Hughes, J. (Writer and director). (1984). *The Breakfast Club.* Los Angeles: Universal Film.

Hurley, D. (1986, July). The hit parade. *Psychology Today,* pp. 22-30.

Inhelder, B., & Piaget, J. (1958). *The growth of logical thinking from childhood to adolescence.* New York: Basic Books.

Jourard, S. M. (1968). *Disclosing man to himself.* Princeton, NJ: Van Nostrand.

Larson, R., & Csikszentmihalyi, M. (1984). *Being adolescent: Conflict and growth in the teenage years.* New York: Basic Books.

Leonhard, C. (1984). The future of musical education in America: A pragmatist's view. In D. Shetler (Ed.), *The future of musical education in America: Proceedings of the July 1983 conference.* Rochester, NY: Eastman School of Music Press.

Mergendeller, J. R., & Mitman, A. L. (1985). The relationship of middle school program features, instructional strategy, instructional performance, and student engagement. *Journal of Early Adolescence 5,* 183-196.

Newman, J. (1985). Adolescents: Why they can be so obnoxious. *Adolescence 20* (79), 635-645.

Purkey, W. W., & Novak, J. M. (1984). *Inviting school success* (2d ed.) Belmont, CA: Wadsworth Publishing.

Renner, J. W., & Stafford, D. G. (1976). The operational levels of secondary school students. In J. W. Renner, D. G. Stafford, A. E. Lawson, J. W. McKinnon, F. E. Friot, & D. H. Kellogg, *Research, teaching and learning with the Piaget model.* Norman: University of Oklahoma Press.

Rice, F. P. (1984). *The adolescent: Development, relationships, and culture.* (4th ed.). Boston: Allyn & Bacon.

Siegel, B. F. (1981, July). *Personally and professionally inviting others.* Paper presented at the Annual Invitational Education Conference, Cullowhee, North Carolina.

Spock, B. (1986, March). Parenting. *Redbook,* pp 23-24.

Treating teens in trouble. (1986, January 20). *Newsweek,* pp. 52-54.

Wapnick, J. (1976). A review of research on attitude and preference. *Council for Research for Music Education,* Bulletin No. 48, pp. 1-19.

Whiteside, M., & Merriman, G. (1976). Dropouts look at their teachers. *Phi Delta Kappan 57,* 700-702.

Why must I be a teenager in love? (popular song). (1959). Pomus (Lyricist), and Shuman (Composer). New York: Unichappel Music.

Advancing from Here

by Charles R. Hoffer

The title for this article was selected for a reason: The matter of music instruction for the more than 80 percent of the high school students who are not enrolled in performing groups is much too important to allow it to fade away after a conference on the topic, no matter how successful that conference may have been. The music instruction of this majority is not just another portion of a desirable music-program. Something deeper is involved here, because reaching and involving these students has to do with what we in the profession of music education are about; it has to do with our "professional soul," if you will.

Are we really in the business of educating people in music? Is the profession of music education mainly interested in the talented performers and those students who are willing to make the large commitments of time and effort that are usually required? Or do school music teachers really want to develop a vital musical culture (which has been an MENC goal for some sixteen years) by educating a greater proportion of the students in music?

If music educators are truly interested in educating students in music, they should be very concerned about the fact that a majority of the students have no music instruction in school after approximately grade seven, which means about the age of twelve or thirteen. If music educators fail to reach a greater share of the students, then their subject will continue to be somewhat on the fringe of the curriculum—and deservedly so. Clearly, music educators need to make a major effort to reach the many high school students not currently in performing groups.

Part of the effort must consist of "carrying the message" to two groups: persons not in music education—school administrators, parents, board members, and others; and the sizable group of music educators who appear to have little interest in music instruction for students who are not performers.

The message to nonmusicians

First, invite the nonmusicians to participate in music studies. The lack of understanding about the purposes and values of music for

31

school students is a major obstacle to the advancement of music education today. The overwhelming majority of persons outside the field tend to think that school music programs exist to provide entertainment at PTA meetings and football games. They further believe that when a group performs well, even if the performance includes only a very limited type of music, it is the mark of a good music program. One result of this situation is that music educators are sometimes not taken very seriously. Part of the reason (but not the entire reason) for this condition can be laid at the doorstep of music educators themselves. As a rule, they have not made an effort to inform others about what they are doing and why they are doing it. They have worked very hard at teaching their students, especially in learning to perform pieces of music, but have neglected to educate others about the value of their instruction for the students.

In 1985 the MENC Southern Division adopted as its special project the development of a publication designed to help music educators inform others about the nature and purposes of music education. That effort is now complete in manuscript form, and it is hoped that it can be published soon.[1] It is, of course, not reasonable to expect busy music teachers to spend several hours each week educating school principals and parents about the reasons for and nature of the music education program. However, a little effort on their part in this area could pay large dividends in terms of improved understanding and support.

The message to professional music teachers

Second, involve other music educators. Several actions can be taken by music educators who are interested in music for the majority of high school students to generate greater support among others in the profession. Articles can be written on the topic for the *Music Educators Journal* and state magazines. A special publication is certainly in order. The logical source for the development of such a book or monograph is the Society for General Music. In addition, sessions on the need for general music courses for high school students should be included in state, division, and national music education conferences. Music teachers need to have suggestions and ideas for instructing the general students more effectively.

Certainly another MENC-sponsored conference on the topic should be held within the next year or two. A single-focus conference is an excellent means of highlighting a particular need. Furthermore, such conferences bring like-minded persons together, and all sorts of good things can happen under those circumstances.

MENC also can recognize those high schools and individuals who have been especially successful in developing programs for the general students. Perhaps awards could be given for outstanding courses, much as are currently awarded for district programs.

---

1. *Beyond the Classroom: Informing Others* is currently available from MENC and can be obtained by contacting Publications Sales at 703-860-4000.

The legislatures and governing boards of education in over twenty states have given music educators a rare opportunity to grow and advance, to move to a greater extent into the mainstream of the high school curriculum. It would be tragic if music educators ignored or bungled this opportunity. My hope and belief is that they will seize on it, and in doing so make a major advance in the promotion of an enlightened musical culture.

This is, indeed, a pretty exciting prospect for the music education profession!

Part II:

Reports of Current Issues and Discussion Groups

Issue 1: Teacher Competencies

Mary Palmer, Discussion Group Leader

Although most music educators are certified to teach all areas of the field in grades K-12, they become narrowly specialized in general, instrumental, or vocal music education. The skills required to teach high school choral groups or elementary general music classes may be very different from those necessary for success with the high school general music student. Since these specializations begin to take shape during the undergraduate years, two primary questions regarding the development of teacher competencies emerged:

1. Are teachers who have been successful instrumental or vocal teachers adequately prepared to teach high school general music? Why or why not?

2. If additional preparation is needed for some teachers to teach high school general music successfully, how can those teachers currently in the field be assisted?

Current inadequacies in teacher education

In his opening address to this conference, MENC President Paul Lehman asserted that college general music methods courses typically emphasize elementary general music to the near exclusion of high school general music. He pointed out that preparation for the secondary level in teacher education needs to be taken more seriously. Lehman emphasized the need for in-service programs for current teachers of high school general music.

It was felt that music educators are not adequately prepared to teach general music at *any* level. There was discussion and speculation as to why this may be the case. Students entering college music education programs often have not considered general music as an area of interest or one worthy of study. Few prospective teachers aspire to become general music practitioners at any level, and especially in the high school.

Many college students view their professional roles as entertainment providers, and consequently choose a music education major in order to become band and show choir directors. Others view teaching as an option to be pursued only by those who cannot or will not become successful performers. For many, teaching general music is the least attractive career option. Such aspirations—or the lack of

37

them—are attitudinal factors that influence career choices and, hence, affect the seriousness that college students assign to courses related to general music education.

It was pointed out that since the field of high school general music is relatively new, university professors may not be adequately prepared to teach such methods courses. It was suggested that college instructors should pilot teach and field test instructional materials in the high school general music classroom. Such an approach would have a dual benefit: The college faculty would establish credibility in this new field and simultaneously would have opportunities to try out new ideas and develop effective materials.

Suggestions for teacher education programs

There was general agreement in this discussion group that adding staff who specialize in general music teaching rather than "retreading" current choral and instrumental music teachers might be the best solution to long-range staffing problems. However, it was believed that the practicality and urgency of the situation dictate that current staff need to be retrained. Additionally, it was recommended that all college secondary school music education majors should follow a two-track curriculum combining either instrumental or choral music teacher preparation with general music. By so doing, students entering the teaching profession would be better prepared to teach in their chosen areas while flexibly and competently adjusting to the changing demands of new course offerings.

Teacher in-service needs

Discussion of other recommendations followed. Developing a list of high school general music clinicians was suggested. Summer study, including participatory hands-on workshops, was encouraged. Such offerings should be advertised in journals most often read by choral and instrumental directors.

Several teachers in this discussion group pointed out the "old-fashionedness" of their own teacher preparation. They voiced a need to help teachers learn more about diverse musical styles and genres, including non-Western musics and twentieth-century techniques. Additional needs emphasizing music education strategies for motivating students and guiding their creative expressions were articulated. Also, teachers need to develop diagnostic and communication skills so they can meet individual students' needs while conveying the art of music. It was pointed out that there are many avenues to success and that teachers must be helped to develop confidence in themselves and their own ideas.

Many members of this group lamented the fact that very few curriculum materials are available for the high school general music program. Specific goals need to be identified and materials to achieve them need to be developed. The publication and sharing of appropriate, quality materials should be encouraged. The foregoing concerns were emphasized as critical to the success of high school general music programs.

Conclusions

The responsibility for developing teachers competent in the area of high school general music is broad. School districts, colleges and universities, professional organizations, and teachers must work together to develop a cadre of teachers who are willing to meet this new challenge. Moreover, those responsible for general music emphases in teacher education programs must equip themselves for teaching these courses and subsequently cultivate interest and expertise in high school general music teaching among their most promising young teachers.

Issue 2: The Impact on Traditional Secondary Music Programs

Avery Glenn, Discussion Group Leader

High school music programs are traditionally performance-oriented. Although instruction for social instruments such as guitar and piano is increasing, the band, chorus, and orchestra still are the cornerstones of secondary music instruction. Some administrators may hire additional instructors for general music, but most will assign any new general music courses to the existing staff. Two primary questions arose that reflect the concerns of professionals with established instructional responsibilities in the high school:

1. How can music teachers be helped to see that the expansion of the music program does not adversely affect traditional performing ensembles?

2. What positive effects can general music instruction have on the traditional music program?

Recommendations for performance-oriented teachers

Music teachers should be encouraged to offer *beginning classes* in band, chorus, and orchestra at the high school level. These classes may consist of small groups of students on like instruments and emphasize playing solos or small ensemble literature rather than large group repertoire.

Instrumental and choral teachers should receive in-service instruction so that they do not feel threatened if required to teach a general music class. Teachers should become "comprehensive music educators" and develop competencies beyond those required of the band, choir, and orchestra director. Teacher education institutions can assist in this effort by revising their undergraduate music education programs to include methods courses or units in general music instruction at the secondary level.

Potential positive outcomes

General music classes in the senior high school can be used to encourage students to continue their music study. Perhaps these courses can serve to encourage students to pursue performing opportunities in traditional large ensembles. In addition, classtime can be creatively used to introduce the music to be performed by bands, choirs, and orchestras in local school concerts. General music classes also may be designed to provide a broad, cultural orientation to music history and music appreciation. What better way is there to educate audiences for future school and community concerts?

The opportunity to teach a general music class may mean that teachers with an insufficient teaching load in band, choir, or orchestra will not need to teach out-of-field subjects such as English, math, or general science. By teaching general music courses, directors of traditional ensembles will be able to remain in the field which they are best qualified to teach.

Issue 3: Motivating Students to Learn in General Music Courses

Nathaniel J. Phipps, Discussion Group Leader

Students who for one reason or another have not opted to be a part of a traditional music program may now be required to take a class in the arts. Often these students are referred to as "the other 80 percent" are the high school general students. The music backgrounds of these students are likely to be very disparate. When compared with students who elect traditional performing ensembles, this segment of the high school population probably will approach music learning with different expectations, needs, and concerns. Therefore, one pertinent question was addressed in this discussion group: What motivational techniques might be used to invite high school general students to elect and enjoy a general music course?

Discussion centered around the three groups believed to be critical to the success of a general music program: teachers, students, and administrators. Members of this discussion group focused on ways in which motivation—or the lack of it—affected these different groups.

The teacher's perspective

Teacher attitude regarding general music was identified as the major contributing factor to the success or failure of the course. Teacher support, therefore, was seen as paramount to the quality and success of the course. The ensuing discussion generated the following list of ways to build teacher commitment and support for a high school general music course:

1. Provide pre- and in-service education specifically addressing the skills necessary to effectively teach a high school general music course. Above all, teachers need to acquire confidence in teaching such courses if they are to avoid feeling defensive or threatened.

2. Provide ample teaching materials including commercial textbooks as well as teacher-developed units and supplementary materials.

3. Equip teaching stations with adequate equipment including LP phonograph or CD playback devices, videotape and audiotape recorders, earphones, and microcomputers.

4. Make available a variety of musical instruments, both recreational and conventional, as well as electronic keyboards, synthesizers, mixers, and amplifiers.

5. Provide adequate space and room assignments (particularly for small-group work) to facilitate the success of the course.

6. Make planning time available for teachers with general music responsibilities.

7. Offer general music teachers sufficient funding to acquire continuing education units or graduate credits for in-service study.

The student's perspective

Members of this discussion group agreed that the teacher should be prepared to start where the students are as a means of motivation. This is not to imply the course should adopt a popular music emphasis, but that music with appeal and the potential for success should be used to generate some measure of initial interest in musical study. In addition, the course should make great use of hands-on, participatory activities such as singing and playing instruments.

Electronic instruments (particularly keyboards) should be an integral part of the program since the level of student interest in this medium is especially high. Students should be provided opportunities to perform both their original works and works of other composers.

The administrator's perspective

Much of what has been identified as basic to a successful program requires administrative support. Therefore, the general music program must be considered as important as the traditional large performing groups not only by teachers, but by all building and district administrators.

Administrators need to be helped to see the value of new general music courses for the nonperforming high school student. Once administrators see the need for and value of such courses, they must enable existing music faculty members to begin the process of curriculum development. In particular, the greatest areas of needed administrative support include:

1. Time and funding for in-service education at seminars, graduate symposia and courses, and special workshops on secondary general music teaching;

2. Summer stipends for music faculty to write curriculum guidelines and actual course materials;

3. Compassion and practical assistance in devising class and rehearsal schedules that will facilitate introducing new music courses;

4. Budgeting assistance to acquire needed instructional resources and equipment.

Members of this discussion group could only speculate about current levels of motivation for general music study from teachers, students, and administrators. There was a strong consensus, however, that students' motivation to take a general music course would correlate directly with administrative support and the individual teacher's interest in teaching such a course.

Issue 4: Learning Outcomes

John Yeager, Discussion Group Leader

Some general music classes are skill-oriented, while others emphasize music appreciation. What the high school general music student should know at the end of a semester or a year of instruction has not been clearly established. Learning strategies for such courses are, therefore, highly varied. The single focus of this discussion group was to address one basic question: What specific learning outcomes are appropriate for high school general music courses?

Desired outcomes from high school general music courses

Throughout the history of general music, course content frequently has been determined by the teacher's musical interests and performance skills. If learning outcomes are to be valid preparation for enriched, lifelong musical encounters, teaching strategies must be based on varied, sequential learning experiences that are appropriate for the general student. It was the consensus of this discussion group that the following are the most important desired learning outcomes:

1. Students will demonstrate attitudinal changes that can result in becoming more discriminating participants and consumers of music.

2. Students will be able to use music vocabulary to describe their affective responses to the manipulation of musical elements in a variety of compositions and musical styles.

3. Students will acquire a basis for making musical judgments and will be able to critique musical performances intelligently.

4. Students will be able to create original compositions for their personal enjoyment, using guidelines developed from Orff, Manhattanville, and other sources.

5. Students will demonstrate an interest in future music study and participation.

If high school general music instruction is to achieve its primary goal—that of enriching the student's life through music—then students must be successful in their musical accomplishments that have meaning in their own lives. Moreover, teachers must be successful in bringing about music learning, and thereby their own satisfaction in teaching the general, nonperformance student. If the basic needs of either students or teachers are not met, then music educators will have failed to meet the challenge of high school general music instruction.

Part III:

Reports of Curriculum Project Teams

Curriculum Emphasis 1: A Performance-Based Approach to High School Music Courses

Hunter March, Project Team Leader

Recent research by Boyer, Goodlad, and Gardner suggests that music instruction should be a basic part of the total school curriculum for all students. Traditionally, music programs have focused only on a small percentage of the school population, but in fact *all* students should have opportunities to experience music through its performance. In the context of high school general music coursework, the process of performing music assists in developing cognitive, affective, and psychomotor skills that are essential to understanding music as an art.

The rationale for a performance-based approach

A performance-based approach for the general music student in high school is important for the following reasons:

1. Music is a communicative art.
2. Music making is essential to a total musical experience.
3. Music performance affords the student an avenue for developing a positive self-image.
4. "Hands-on" experiences are thought to be highly motivating and essential to a comprehensive understanding of music.
5. In performing, students experience a synthesis of all the elements of music.
6. Performance enriches the aesthetic experience.
7. Performance provides the immediate opportunity to analyze, evaluate, and think critically about music.

Through a course emphasizing exploration of various performing media, students are encouraged to be more than just consumers of music. Participation in an active musical experience promotes involvement in music as a lifelong opportunity and provides an outlet for enrichment and creative expression through performance. A course of this nature should encourage self-directed, creative growth.

Curriculum Emphasis 2: A Listening-Based Approach to High School Music Courses

Rebecca Silverstein and John Yeager,
Project Team Leaders

High school general music may be the last formal music instruction received by nonperformance-oriented music students. Many avenues of experiencing music should be explored by these students. A primary goal of listening-based instruction is to develop informed, discriminating consumers of music for the future. Well-planned listening activities should be the primary aspect of general music study and should provide the focal point for developing such courses.

Desired outcomes of a listening-based approach

Through directed, participatory listening experiences, students will be able to demonstrate the following musical behaviors:

1. Experience and demonstrate an understanding of musical compositions and styles that are beyond their performance abilities.

2. Focus on, identify, and respond to specific musical concepts as used in a wide spectrum of musical cultures and styles.

3. Demonstrate understanding that will enable them to move from known music to unknown to the "new known" by comparing and contrasting the musical components that selected works contain in common.

4. Identify ways in which individuals, groups, and cultures use music.

5. Demonstrate broadened musical interests and expanded musical values regarding a wide variety of music from traditional and nontraditional sound sources.

6. Demonstrate an ability to perceive and evaluate music meaningfully.

Curriculum Emphasis 3: An Arts-Based Approach to High School Music Courses

Frances Ulrich, Project Team Leader

An arts-based general music course is one in which music instruction is aligned with and illuminated by visual art, dance, and theater. The following rationale, desired outcomes, and suggested approaches are designed to assist educators in planning for senior high school general music courses.

Rationale

In the words of Ernest Boyer, President of the Carnegie Foundation for the Advancement of Teaching, "The arts are an essential part of the human experience.... From the dawn of civilization, men and women have used music, dance, theater, and the visual arts to transmit the heritage of a people and express human joys and sorrows. They are the means by which a civilization can be measured" (Boyer, 1983).

Boyer's view of the arts helps to emphasize the role of aesthetic education in our daily lives. Collectively, the arts share a common purpose and responsibility in the high school curriculum. Cultivating students' abilities to perceive the unique characteristics of the arts is a requirement for experiencing the expressive nature of dance, drama, visual art, and music. Therefore, the *education of perception* must be a basic part of curricula designed for individuals of any age.

An arts-based general music curriculum provides diverse media through which one may refine aesthetic perceptions. Offering different media and modes of learning that accommodate individual preferences and learning styles, an arts-based curriculum supports the development of aesthetic responsiveness by providing many experiences through which perception may be cultivated. An arts-based curriculum serves to broaden the potential for responding to the power of all the arts as creative expressions of human beings.

Desired outcomes of an arts-based curriculum

As a result of study in an arts-based curriculum, high school students should be able to demonstrate the following skills and understandings:

49

1. Exhibit an understanding of artistic principles (such as unity, variety, repetition, variation) and their commonality among the arts.

2. Differentiate the unique qualities and elements present among different art forms.

3. Apply a general knowledge of stylistic characteristics of the major periods in the world's artistic history and in American artistic culture when making artistic decisions.

4. Discuss the ways and means by which the arts serve humanity.

5. Make informed aesthetic judgments based on accepted criteria that will serve as reference points for such judgments throughout one's adult life.

Members of this discussion group were unable to reach a consensus about all desired outcomes. There was considerable debate, for example, about statement number three. Many in the group believed that this outcome should be divided into two major and discrete outcomes:

1. Acquire a basic understanding of the arts that are specifically indigenous to *American* artistic culture; and

2. Demonstrate a familiarity with the stylistic characteristics of the major periods of creative aesthetic endeavors in *world* history.

Suggested approaches for arts-based course organization

An arts-based general music curriculum in the high school could be organized according to any one of the following recommended themes:

1. By artistic principle (for example, contrast, balance, unity, and variety);

2. By chronology among all the arts or within individual art forms;

3. By broader trends in artistic styles and periods (for example, Baroque, Impressionist, Dada, and avant-garde);

4. By topical themes (for example, brotherhood, war and peace, religious celebrations, love and romance, and nationalism); or

5. By role perception (through directed participation as composers, painters, dancers, actors).

Reference
Boyer, E. L. (1983). *High school: A report on secondary education in America.* New York: Harper and Row.

Curriculum Emphasis 4: A Comprehensive Approach to High School Music Courses

Phyllis Dorman and Russell Robinson,
Project Team Leaders

A comprehensive approach to high school general music suggests an eclectic view of secondary music courses. In some ways, this approach combines traditional general music teaching techniques (similar to those found in earlier grades) with an emphasis on personalizing music learning experiences so that acquired skills and knowledge will carry over into young adulthood. Potential course titles using this approach might be: Personal Musicianship; Music Perspectives; Music Making I; and Musical Horizons.

The rationale for a comprehensive general music approach

A course based on a comprehensive view of music and musicianship represents a viable approach for all high school students because:

1. It provides an overview of what it means to function musically; that is, to function as a composer, a listener, or a performer.

2. It may be built on the existing general music program offered at the elementary and junior high or middle school levels. Obviously, such a course would represent an extension of these earlier experiences.

3. It is flexible and easily adaptable to varied school populations, ethnic backgrounds, socioeconomic conditions, and community traditions.

4. It provides for a balance and a variety in the types of musical behaviors and skills brought to the class by students.

5. It emphasizes creative, active involvement in music making.

6. It can incorporate a variety of musical media such as choral groups, percussion ensembles, electronic instruments, guitars, keyboards, and ensembles with mixed instrumentation.

7. It allows for the diversity necessary to develop critical thinking and musical taste.

Basic goals of a comprehensive general music approach

As a result of taking a traditional comprehensive general music course, high school students should be able to do the following:

1. Analyze musical properties such as structure, melody, instrumentation, or rhythm, and describe these verbally.

2. Use appropriate vocabulary when encountering and participating in new musical experiences.

3. Identify similarities and differences in and between compositions.

4. Make musical choices based on intellectual understanding as well as on emotional or social factors.

5. Show respect and openness for music of varied cultures, genres, periods, and styles.

6. Make value judgments on musical performances based on a comprehensive knowledge of music literature and technical performing skills.

7. Choose music for personal listening that might not have been chosen before having the experiences in the course.

8. Conduct an ensemble with appropriate entrances, cutoffs, and expressive controls in both metrical and ametrical compositions or improvisations.

9. Play simple accompaniments on keyboard and folk instruments.

10. Play from notation and improvise on keyboard and folk instruments.

11. Participate in group or solo singing of varied styles of music literature.

12. Respond to music with structured and improvisatory movement.

13. Execute physical representations of music sounds and symbols such as Kodály hand signals and stem notation.

14. Create music compositions that challenge and reflect acquired music performance skills.

Desired outcomes of a comprehensive general music approach

As a result of their study in a comprehensive general music course, it is hoped that high school students will be able to:

1. Exhibit increased positive responses to all types of music.

2. Feel comfortable expressing themselves through sound, improvising and performing vocally and on selected instruments.

3. Share their creative efforts with peers and respond positively to the musical efforts of other students.

4. Use music as a source of aesthetic fulfillment.

Part IV:

Workshops in Teaching General Music

Bridging the Gap from the Podium to the High School General Music Class Using Concert Percussion

by Lenore Pogonowski

Many adults I meet wish they could play a musical instrument and regret they didn't have the opportunity to do so when they were growing up. I have a hunch that most nonperforming high school students also have a secret desire to play an instrument. But, if they haven't done so by the time they are sophomores and juniors, chances are, they don't see themselves capable of doing it.

If general music could be transformed into a living, interactive experience, more high school students might carry music making with them into their adult lives. The general music requirement at the high school level offers a new opportunity for engaging many more students as participants in music. It is probably the last chance we have for cultivating positive attitudes toward musical participation in an otherwise disinterested population.

This article provides an approach for teaching music to high school general music students that capitalizes on their basic needs to be actively involved and socially interactive. It demonstrates how conductors of performing organizations model musical behavior as a means for engaging nonperformers in the act of making and learning about music. Following a description of the approach, strategies for implementation are discussed.

One of the first things music educators must do is convince students that this is going to be a "different" kind of class, rather than one more instructional attempt to merely make them literate about musical notation or the classical repertoire. They are not going to sit and passively take notes. All class members should be musically involved so that musical experience creates the *need* for instruction and so that the two go hand in hand.

Getting started: Suggestions for the first day of class

We convince the students of this intention by what we do in class from the very first day. If we spend too much time telling them what the class is going to be about, we risk losing their confidence at the outset. Students must somehow taste the flavor of what is in store for them as soon as possible and that flavor should be one that piques their interest.

Personalizing the environment goes a long way in breaking down initial barriers that prevent open sharing or trusting relationships in the music-making experience. A strategy that I have found to be successful is one that requires the students to share something about themselves that relates to music. Students find someone in the class they don't know and introduce themselves with the information. Some examples of what I have asked students to think about and then share during the introductions are: (1) The recollection of the first time they were turned on by a musical event. Why or how were they turned on? (2) What is their greatest fear about music? and (3) If the president of the United States ordered that everyone in our society play an instrument, which one would they choose? Why?

Following the initial pairing and introductions, I suggest they find two other people and introduce each other to the new people and vice versa. By the time this is accomplished (ten or fifteen minutes) there is a lot of conversation going on among the students. More important, they have taken their first steps away from self-consciousness and toward working together as a musical team.

While this activity may take approximately twenty minutes of this important first class, it is valuable because it addresses the social or peer orientation that is so much a part of high school students. It communicates something about us as teachers, as well. Our focus on students as people suggests that we are not so caught up in subject matter as to forget who makes up the membership in our classes.

Building anticipation for general music class

With the preliminaries behind us in the first fifteen or twenty minutes of the class, we are ready to embark on our musical strategy. Let's consider for a moment what the students already sensed as they entered a room that heretofore was reserved for band and orchestra students. The room has been carefully planned for them with each concert percussion instrument in its own space rather than bunched up in the corner where the band and orchestra percussionists generally stand. An audio system with microphones also commands its own area not too far from the podium. The room is filled with a sense of anticipation or anxiety depending upon the student's predisposition to general music class.

There are many musical strategy options one can exercise as a beginning, but I usually decide to focus on rhythm. I begin by assuming that all students have, at some point or another, observed percussionists in performance, and therefore have a sense of how the instruments work. The students are invited to assume positions with the instruments even though I know most of them will not necessarily hold their beaters or the instruments in a precisely correct way. I treat them as seasoned performers and speak up to their earned level of maturity—and they are aware and responsive to both, and terribly curious. Also, I know that I will have many opportunities to assist them in the proper handling of mallets once the real business of what we are about in this class gets digested.

Options for immediate performance

At this point there are at least two options for proceeding with the strategy. One option is to tell the students we are going to create an aleatory composition—a composition based on chance. Their requirements as performers are to listen carefully to the musical responses of others as well as their own and to maintain eye contact as much as possible with the teacher as conductor so that they will know when to enter and exit the piece with the approximate volume level expected from them. Without a preconceived idea of what they will play when cued, students' attention is directed to the evolving piece and not distracted with trying to remember a particular rhythmical idea and how it's going to fit in. The advantage of this option is its spontaneity.

A second option is to provide the students with two or three minutes to explore some potential rhythms they could use in response to a conductor's cue in an aleatory composition. The advantage of this option is two-fold: (1) The teacher can listen to each student and have some idea what they will perform when cued, and (2) analytical listening to the similarities and differences of their responses can serve as a focus for an ensuing dialogue. Both options serve as viable beginnings and each can be tried on separate occasions.

Conducting and performing the first piece

With one of the options having been determined, the teacher now assumes the role of conductor just as if the band, orchestra, or chorus were in front of him. The conductor, or one of the students, triggers the record mechanism on the tape recorder, and the piece begins...with silence...until every eye makes unison contact with his. A triangle enters upon cue and the conductor, through his nonverbal communication, plays with its sound against the silence of the room. A single sound is allowed to fade, rapid reiterations are indicated in the dynamic shape of a *crescendo*, and no particular meter has yet been established. The conductor's attention gravitates to the bass drum indicating a *pianissimo* entrance of a sort. With nodding approval, the conductor invites the bass drum performer to continue, with slight *crescendi* and *diminuendi* to generate energy. While this is going on there also have been some occasional references back to the triangle. Over the continuing bass drum part (which more or less settles into an ostinato as an outcome of continuous repetition), a shaking tambourine is cued in and followed by a similar cue to the maracas. A musical dialogue between tambourine and maracas is shaped by the conductor's cues. Gradually, other such dialogues between different instruments are created until all the students at instruments are involved in the chance piece. In all probability the piece has settled into a regular meter at this point. The conductor can now play up the drama of changing dynamics, sudden silences, and feature new combinations of instruments for musical dialogue within the framework of the entire piece.

How long does it last? Does it end with a single triangle as it began? What chance factor suddenly alerts the conductor that an ending is in sight? The answers to these questions will be different every time and so will the piece. But, the unpredictability of a chance piece is the very thing that generates musical excitement and serves as a basis for discussions about how music works. It is the experience of music making together that elevates the need for instruction in the students' eyes. The teacher and the students are sharing in a way that makes success for anyone contingent on the efforts of everyone.

Involving students in musical analysis and evaluation

The goal following the piece is to get students involved in analysis and evaluation as a positive means for growth so they begin to see their potential ability in and sensitivity to the making of music. To promote awareness and discussion, we listen to the tape recording that has been made of the chance piece. At this early stage in the semester we invite the students to identify aspects of the piece they felt were successful, and more specifically, what contributed to those moments of success. We also discuss alternative ways in which the piece might go during another occasion with perhaps one of the students as the conductor.

As preparation for a new piece, the timbral range of the instruments and the techniques for producing sounds on them are explored. In a follow-up class, students in pairs can sample all the instruments on a rotating basis to make note of the number of different sounds available to them on the instruments. This exercise in divergent thinking forces performance considerations beyond the obvious uses of the instruments. As the teacher moves from dyad to dyad observing the students' work, it also affords casual opportunities to make suggestions regarding hand positions, use of mallets, or other instructional aides that will facilitate sound production and technique development. Additionally, it extends the range of performing options that students will have available in their future group music-making efforts.

Creating a nonthreatening learning environment

Now that students are more knowledgeable about the instruments and their performing options, the teacher can solicit volunteer conductors for the next aleatory pieces. Students can work individually or they can collaborate on a plan, then decide which one of them will conduct it. I generally suggest that they have a good idea about how they are going to start the piece and have some thoughts about what constitutes an ending even though any preconceived thoughts they have of the ending may change as the piece progresses.

We participate as performers, then tape record and listen to several aleatory pieces by student conductors. Their performances in and observations about the pieces become more and more astute as their ears begin to hear subtleties that previously went unnoticed. Students become less and less self-conscious as the level of commitment to the class and the musical success of the pieces increases. If all of this has taken place in a nonthreatening but challenging environment, the students are ready for instruction that will raise the level of the challenge yet not stifle the momentum that has been accomplished.

Inviting creative thinking

In the same inductive manner by which we led the students in discussions of the pieces, we explore the ways in which we could vary a particular rhythm. For example, after performing the eighth-note pattern as written below, invite students to suggest variations based on it through demonstration.

Create an ongoing list of variation treatments through the introduction of appropriate musical symbols as they are demonstrated in performance. Extend student suggestions to include considerations for (1) dynamics, (2) use of silence, (3) tempo, (4) accents, and (5) time, (for example, tied notes for longer durations). Examples of what they might suggest are as follows.

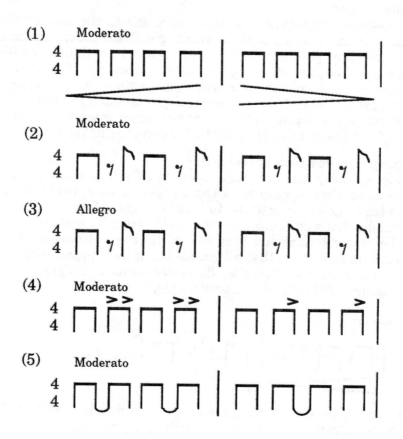

These examples are only approximations of what the students will suggest. I think it is important to notate their ideas for them because it lends prestige to their musical thinking and reinforces in standard notation what they are rendering in sound. They are more apt to practice the notated examples of what they have personally volunteered than a given set of teacher-prepared variation treatments or rhythmic patterns. Using their contributions (and thereby honoring the personal investment they make in their class) will go a long way in developing positive attitudes. It is vital that we have students know we are truly interested in their musical thinking.

Using students' musical ideas in improvisations

With a number of alternatives notated on the chalkboard, engage the entire class in an extemporaneous improvisation based on any of the ideas suggested thus far. Let them select from the list of notated musical alternatives what they will play when cued by the conductor. Invite them to select their choices based on what they hear going on around them. A rule of thumb for maintaining spontaneity and experimentation with additional rhythmical variations is to offer students the option of occasionally making up new patterns during the course of the improvisation.

The large-group improvisational framework affords the teacher the opportunity to refine a variety of skills. Working with the group, teachers can provide practice opportunities for students who have difficulty with certain rhythms. Periodic *tutti* unison responses, when cued by the conductor during the course of an improvisation, can assist students in refining performance skills of rhythms they find problematic. Practice with notational skills is also accomplished since the teacher or student conductor would refer to the notation of these rhythms on the chalkboard.

Small-group composition activities

Small-group compositional work is an equally important component of the class. Small-group work can be seen as an opportunity to synthesize the large-group activity. In small groups of four or five students, the individuals determine the musical context by making all or most of the musical decisions that will affect the outcome of their pieces. I sometimes suggest that all groups begin their pieces with the same rhythmic motive so that they can later compare differences in the continuations of their pieces. For example,

When the pieces are completed, we tape record them for immediate playback reference. The tape recording accomplishes several

objectives. First, it acknowledges the importance of their work by taking the time to play it back. Second, the recording gives the performers an opportunity to listen to their piece without the moment-to-moment concerns of live performance. Third, it provides an aural catalog that can be returned to when clarification in a discussion requires it. Fourth, it can be put in the library or some other accessible place where students can choose to listen to it outside of class.

The small-group pieces serve as a springboard for repeating the strategies discussed thus far. Cue sheets based on an increasingly growing list of notated rhythmical events can be prepared and utilized as scores in large-group improvisations. The list of rhythmical events can be further enhanced by listening to professional percussion ensemble recordings. With access to a relatively inexpensive rhythm synthesizer, students can generate more complex rhythms upon which to build their own pieces as well as receive notational feedback of those rhythms in visual form.

Summary

Bridging the gap from the podium to the high school general music class can be accomplished through the use of concert percussion. The challenge is to combine musical experience with music instruction in such a way that the meaning and reasoning behind the instruction grows out of the experience. When the music/instruction experience capitalizes on the high school student's needs to be actively involved and socially interactive, we take our first big step in meeting this challenge. One of the strongest bonds between the high school student and the general music class is the feeling of productive participation that is shared in the making of a musical composition.

Selected listening examples

Antheil, George. *Ballet Mécanique*. Urania UX134.
Bartók, Béla. *Concerto for Two Pianos, Percussion and Orchestra*. Columbia MS6956.
Bartók, Béla. *Music for Strings, Percussion and Celesta*. Capital P8299.
Cage, John et al. *Concert Percussion*. Time 58000.
Chavez, Carlos. *Toccata for Percussion*. Capital P8299.
Goodman, Saul. *Canon for Percussion*. Columbia CL1533.
Goodman, Saul. *Timpiana*. Columbia CL1533.
Gould, Morton. *Parade*. Columbia CL1533.
Hovhanness, Alan. *October Mountain*. Urania UX134.
LoPresti, Ronald. *Sketch for Percussion*. Urania UX134.
Milhaud, Darius. *Concerto for Percussion and Small Orchestra*. Capital P8299.
Partch, Harry. *Daphne of the Dunes*. Columbia MS7207.
Partch, Harry. *Castor and Pollux*. Columbia MS7207.
Partch, Harry. *Cloud Chamber Music*. CRI 193.
Riley, Terry. *In C*. Columbia MS7178.

Starer, Robert. *Night Music for Percussion*. Columbia CL1533.

Varese, Edgar. *Ionisation*. Columbia ML5478.

Selected readings

Paynter, John. *Music in the Secondary School Curriculum*. New York: Cambridge University Press, 1982.

Paynter, John, and Peter Aston. *Sound and Silence: Classroom Projects in Creative Music*. New York: Cambridge University Press, 1970.

Pogonowski, Lenore. "The Anatomy of a Creative Music Strategy." *Soundings* 3, no. 1, Fall 1983.

Regelski, Thomas. *Teaching General Music: Action Learning for Middle and Secondary Schools*. New York: Schirmer Books, 1981.

Schafer, R. Murray. *Creative Music Education*. New York: Schirmer/Macmillan, 1976.

Thomas, Ronald. *Manhattanville Music Curriculum Program (MMCP) Synthesis*. Bardonia, New York: Media Materials, 1971.

Suggested Setup for Conducted Improvisations

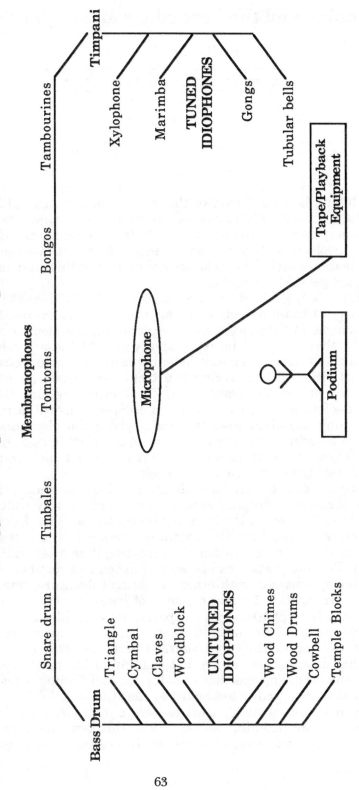

Listening and the Secondary Music Curriculum

by Donald Gingrich

Listening is a vital part of the general music curriculum in the secondary schools. While a small percentage of students in these classes may become active participants in music-making, *all* of them will be involved with music as listeners. Hence it is essential that music teachers strive to make listening an exciting and interesting part of the general music class.

The primary goal for listening at any level is to increase students' sensitivity to those aspects of music that make it expressive. Thus, the emphasis in listening always is placed on the elements of music and how they are used in expressive ways. At the secondary level, such an emphasis implies that listening lessons should focus on three basic activities: (1) analyzing the treatment given an element of music in a particular composition; (2) determining how the various elements of a piece are combined and ordered (musical form); and (3) determining the distinctive treatment given the elements by composers in a particular era or in the music of a certain culture (musical style). These three areas should represent the major emphases of music listening in the secondary schools.

Since listening by nature is often a passive experience, it is essential for the teacher to plan experiences in such a way that students are actively involved in the listening process. One of the keys to active listening is to integrate the listening portion of the class into the other musical activities, rather than treating it as a separate, isolated activity. This integration can be accomplished in a number of ways by (1) involving students with other art forms (literature, dance, visual arts) as preparation for the moment of listening; (2) providing students with the opportunity to experiment with ideas and concepts that later will be encountered in the listening experience (creative problem solving or the "do-it-yourself-first" approach); (3) planning ways that listening will evolve naturally from the performance experience; and (4) giving specifics to listen for and finding ways to determine that these specifics are heard by the students.

The teaching strategy that follows emphasizes a related arts approach to the listening lesson. While this represents only one of several ways to teach music listening, the related arts approach can be one of the most interesting and purposeful means for involving secondary students in music listening. It is a particularly useful approach to the study of musical style. The inclusion of visual art examples in this teaching strategy helps to broaden the students' experiences, and at the same time clarifies musical concepts.

Model strategy

Musical emphasis:	Impressionistic style
Previous experience:	Students have heard and discussed examples of nineteenth-century Romantic realism in the works of Berlioz and Strauss
Approaches:	Related arts and creative problem solving
Materials:	A variety of reflecting surfaces (mirrors, aluminum foil, other surfaces that create vague or distorted images). Slides or prints of Monet's "Waterloo Bridge—Sun in Fog," and Corbet, "Beach at Etretat." Classroom percussion instruments including triangles, finger cymbals, maracas, Autoharps, metallophones, and other mallet percussion. Keyboard instruments prearranged in the whole-tone scale. A recording of Debussy's "Play of the Waves" from *La Mer*.

Suggested learning sequence

I. Preparation (through visual art activities)

    A. View images in a number of reflecting surfaces (mirrors, foil, and so on) and describe these images with basic vocabulary (realistic, distorted, vague, or distinct)

    B. View two works of art: Corbet's "Beach at Etretat" and Monet's "Waterloo Bridge—Sun in Fog."

        1. Relate each work to previous experience with descriptions of images in reflected surfaces.

        2. Expand vocabulary by identifying appropriate adjectives for each art work.

        3. Describe how the effect is created in each work; emphasize color, line, shape, design.

    C. Information: Review goals, ideals of Impressionism in visual art.

II. Musical preparation

    A. Romantic realism and its relationship to Impressionism: Set the aesthetic and historical scene.

    B. Problem: Recreate the atmosphere of the Monet painting in sounds.

1. Choose subtle colors.
2. Establish whole-tone pattern on the bells and improvise on other instruments. Determine a beginning and an ending. Improvise middle section.
3. Perform the composition.
4. Evaluate the choice of colors, treatment of rhythm, dynamics, and melody.

III. Listening to *La Mer*
   A. Give background information about the composition.
   B. Introductory listening
      1. Close your eyes and capture the subtle feeling of a constantly changing sea.
      2. Discover sounds or techniques in *La Mer* that are similar to those used in previous class improvisations.
   C. Draw comparisons between visual and musical effects.
   D. Detailed listening: Use the following guide to focus perception of specific elements.

Listening guide
La Mer by Claude Debussy (1862-1918)

Before listening to the music, read the following descriptive statements. As you listen, decide which statements under each musical component *most clearly* describe the treatment Debussy has used in this music.

I. Timbre (orchestral color)
   A. Emphasizes mostly the muted timbres (colors) of the orchestra.
   B. Emphasizes the brilliant timbres of the orchestra.

II. Melody
   A. Employs several short, motive-like melodies.
   B. Employs several long, lyrical melodies.

III. Rhythm
   A. Features a strongly metrical, driving rhythm.
   B. Features a subtle, indefinite beat.

IV. Dynamics
   A. Stresses low dynamic levels more than high dynamic levels.
   B. Moves constantly toward a brilliant climax.
   C. Achieves several small climaxes but is rarely brilliant.

Problems for further listening
A. Identify the percussion instruments you hear in the music.
B. Hear the whole-tone scale and name the instrument that performs it.
C. Identify anything in the music that reminds you of the previous classroom impressionistic improvisation.

66

Using the Synthesizer in Creating, Composing, and Improvising

by Don Muro

Synthesizers have become the foundation of a large segment of contemporary music. Rapid advancements in music technology have dramatically changed the way musicians compare, arrange, perform, record, and listen to music. Currently, synthesizers are beginning to find their way into general music classrooms, and teachers report a high degree of motivation among students who have the opportunity to use them.

Educators may want to consider the following guidelines when purchasing a synthesizer:

1. In most cases a keyboard synthesizer is preferable to a synthesizer card (or DAC board) that is inserted into a microcomputer. Although DAC boards are quite compact and are very useful for music theory software, they have the following disadvantages:

   a. At the present time, DAC boards cannot match the sonic quality of a dedicated keyboard synthesizer.
   b. Students must learn about microcomputers before learning about synthesizers.
   c. Students equate synthesizer music with computer programming.
   d. Only software that has been written specifically for each DAC board can be used.

Keyboard synthesizers offer the following advantages:

   a. They have an extremely wide variety of potential sounds.
   b. They can be used both as a teaching tool and as a professional musical instrument.
   c. They generate instant student motivation not only through the clavier, but also because students show high interest in both technology and music.
   d. They can be connected (through MIDI technology) to a microcomputer.

2. Although there are many types of synthesizers available, there is no such thing as the "best" synthesizer. An expensive synthesizer

with many subtle features may be inappropriate for teaching the basic concepts of synthesis to a general music student.

3. In most cases, it is better to purchase two or three less expensive synthesizers with fewer features than to buy one expensive instrument with features that will not be used by students.

4. A synthesizer that will be used both as a teaching tool in the classroom and as a musical instrument with performing ensembles should have a full-sized keyboard. Although miniature keyboards are less expensive than full-sized instruments, these smaller synthesizers are virtually unplayable by keyboardists. In addition, miniature keyboards may contribute to the perception of the synthesizer as a toy instead of a professional musical instrument. Quite frequently, these miniature synthesizers are "slaved" to either a full-sized master keyboard or to a microcomputer, thereby eliminating the need to play the miniature instrument.

5. The synthesizer should be equipped with MIDI—Music Instrument Digital Interface. This interface makes it possible to connect the synthesizer to other synthesizers and, most important, to microcomputers.

High school teachers should also consider purchasing a rhythm (or drum) synthesizer for classroom use. Drum synthesizers can be used by themselves or with a microcomputer to introduce and reinforce rhythmic concepts. They also can be used to accompany student compositions or arrangements.

It is important to play keyboard and rhythm synthesizers through a full-range sound system such as a high-fidelity, component audio system. Guitar and bass amplifiers should be used only when no better system is available. These amplifiers cannot reproduce the frequency range of a synthesizer and will yield an undefined and harsh sound. Audio systems produce better sound without harming the speakers. Frequency response and definition, not loudness, are the keys in the classroom. (If an audio system is unavailable, consider buying specially designed compact speakers for synthesizer amplification.)

Teaching strategies

The more synthesizers that are available in the classroom, the more opportunities students will have for hands-on experience. It is possible, however, for students to learn a great deal about the synthesizer with only one instrument in the classroom. Charts, diagrams, front-panel facsimiles, and other handouts can be used to show students the layout and operations of a particular instrument. Students then can be called upon either individually or in small groups to locate specific controls, to change various parameters of a sound, or to play simple musical examples on the keyboard.

Many more options are available to students when the synthesizer is connected (via MIDI) to a microcomputer. With the appropriate software, the microcomputer can act as a "tapeless" recorder. This software allows students to play melodies and chords on the keyboard at a very slow tempo and then program the computer to play the music back at any speed or in any key signature. It is also possible for students to enter notes on the computer keyboard and then hear these notes played back on the synthesizer.

In large classes, students can be divided into groups or teams. Each team would be assigned to compose or arrange a simple piece for the synthesizer and drum computer. Such a team might be composed of the following components: (1) a performer (someone with minimal keyboard skills who can type the notes on a computer keyboard); (2) a computer operator (someone to activate the record and playback modes and the track assignments for each part); (3) a synthesizer sound designer (someone to select synthesizer sounds and effects for each part); and (4) a lyricist (someone who can add lyrics to an instrumental line).

There can be many variations on the previous example, depending on class size and the skills of each student.

Important concepts

It is important for students to understand these synthesizer concepts: (1) Synthesizers are neither easier nor more difficult to play well than any other musical instrument (2) Synthesizers are not exclusively keyboard instruments (guitar and drum synthesizers abound, and interfaces for using any instrument with synthesizer are readily available); and (3) unlike almost every other musical instrument, synthesizers are still changing and developing as musical instruments. As technology advances, synthesizers will become even more powerful and intriguing.

Combining Technology with Creativity in the General Music Class

by Anne D. Modugno

The students from one of the general music classes are discussing a melody written by one of their peers. "I would change the filter for more resonance." "Have you tried preset five?" "Would you consider adding a different waveform to your B section?"

These Music Major II students are sitting in front of a computer synthesizer. Their assignment is to create a melody, put it on the computer synthesizer, and listen to it while altering the tempo, timbre, key, and balance—all of which can be done instantly. By experimenting with the filters, the presets, and the waveforms, they can change the sound from flutelike to one that is bizarre and abstract.

These students have been trained on traditional instruments using traditional notation. They are not only fascinated with the capabilities of the MIDI equipment but are being challenged by all the possibilities that are available to them.

MIDI (Musical Instrument Digital Interface) has invaded the music world. It permits keyboards, drums, sequencers, and computers to "talk to each other." All MIDI equipment is compatible regardless of the manufacturer. These instruments are very much a part of this generation and will probably be basic to future generations. MIDI electronic keyboards currently can be purchased for under $300.

Computer synthesized music, with its multitude of modifications and diverse sounds, is a contemporary idiom that can foster creative activity at any age level. The student is not intimidated by the traditional problems of having to read and understand musical notation. Electronic music is not restricted to clefs, key signatures, and note values. Yet, it is an art that demands imagination, develops the students' desire and ability to explore and investigate new ideas, and challenges him or her to use newly acquired knowledge in a new venture. Students learn to think, to explore, to discover, to be wrong, to be right.

As music teachers, we have a responsibility to create an environment that will stimulate and motivate all interested students. We must introduce new technology, encourage and give students opportunities to explore and experiment with new ideas, and continually give guidance and positive reinforcement.

A healthy, competitive atmosphere can be created using a listening and discussion technique. Questions on the sound sources and modifiers and discussion on form help build aural perception as well as a working musical vocabulary. Instructors should encourage class discussion about compositions. Constructive criticism and self-evaluation help students develop a better understanding of structure and other aspects of the music composition process. Students may talk about tension, relaxation, repetition, contrast, texture, and timbre. What is exciting is that they will bring in unfinished works to get suggestions and criticism from their peers. This shows the students' growing confidence and maturity.

Sustaining a stimulating environment in which students are encouraged and given opportunities to explore and experiment with new ideas is not an easy task. It takes extensive planning and constant evaluation by the instructor. The teacher must stimulate inductive thinking, get all students actively involved, and guide and assist students toward a rewarding musical experience. In turn, the students must use deductive reasoning when evaluating each others' work and should develop a confidence in their own work.

Electronic music that engages computers and MIDI synthesizers encourages students to be creative and involves them in "thinking sound." Through the contemporary medium of this equipment, students become involved as creators. They get immediate response when using preset patterns or "real time" on the drum machine and can have a positive experience creating simple or complex rhythm patterns.

Students can play simple melodies on the keyboard changing presets that alter timbre. They can create abstract sounds as well as imitate traditional instruments.

General music curriculum structure

Students in the general music program at Greenwich High School, Greenwich, Connecticut, have been introduced to these instruments. Offerings in the general music program include Music Major I, II, and III; Electronic Music; Advanced Electronic/Computer Music; Piano; and Guitar.

Both Music Major and Electronic/Computer Music students meet six times in a seven-day cycle. Many students can only schedule three classes in the seven-day cycle because of other academic pressures. To accommodate these variables in the schedule the teacher must plan extensively. New schedules were developed to attract a cross-section of students interested in fulfilling the fine arts requirement.

In a Music Major class, which is an elective in the general music program, the first assignment is to create a melody that can be realized on a computer, a synthesizer, or a traditional instrument.

71

Students with little or no facility on a keyboard or other instruments, turn to the computer to create their melodies. Students with some keyboard facility will use a software program that uses two voices in both the G and F clefs. As the notes appear on the staff, each can be heard as well as seen. The student can associate the pitch with its notated position on the staff. Students who have some musical understanding but little keyboard facility find this program a satisfying, rewarding experience. Students with keyboard skills use the keyboard synthesizer, a more sophisticated piece of equipment.

Electronic Music is another elective in the general music program. Students experiment with the keyboard and drum synthesizers. As they are introduced step-by-step to each piece of equipment, they complete an assignment using that specific instrument. All assignments follow a format: (1) demonstration of equipment for assignment; (2) presentation of the assignment (project) in class; and (3) class evaluation of the project.

The students are responsible for several projects. The projects include (1) creating an eight-bar rhythm pattern on the drum machine; (2) creating a sixteen-measure melody on the keyboard and a rhythm pattern on the drum machine; (3) writing a thirty-second commercial using words plus the MIDI equipment; (4) writing a poem, short story, or one-act play, then writing a sound track that enhances the words; and (5) creating a space, planet, or water odyssey.

The general music program at Greenwich High School has been able to maintain the number of students enrolled in its courses while competing with the increase in the academic base of the students' schedules. To complement their classwork, students use lab time before, during, and after school to complete their assignments. The lab often is occupied until early evening, five days per week!

Computer and synthesizer music combined with creative courses are vital parts of the total music program. They allow for exploration, experimentation, and inductive and deductive reasoning.

Student ability and creativity

All students have creative ability and face the dilemma of every composer in their attempts to manipulate sound in a meaningful way. Students at different musical levels and in different age groups have responded positively and aesthetically to composition using computers and synthesizers as creative instruments.

This creativity is an outgrowth of being involved, and being motivated by the enthusiasm conveyed by the teacher and by fellow students sharing ideas to gain positive recognition.

Motivation is the result of a stimulating environment—an environment that encourages both highly talented and less motivated students to explore, to experiment, to discover, to discuss, and to evaluate.

72

The Transfer from Rock Videos to General Music Videos

by Robert A. Cutietta

Rock videos have become a major musical force in the life of a large number of high school students. In fact, they are becoming frequent musical resources for a growing number of music teachers as well. When I asked you earlier in my demonstration how many of you had seen at least three videos in the past month, many hands were raised.

Over the past few years, rock videos have received massive attention in the media. Many articles have appeared warning parents about the harmful effects of videos. These warnings are warranted in some cases. Regretfully, some videos portray extreme violence; others are abusive to women.

It is vitally important to separate specific, objectionable videos from the general category of "videos." There are many good videos. The medium itself is not destructive; however, the way some artists use the medium is appalling. Videos are no different in this respect than other media. Some books, for example, are trivial, trashy, or pornographic, but not all books are bad. It would be inconceivable to ban books from schools because some are of poor quality. Similarly, we must not ban videos from our general music classes lest we cheat ourselves of a potentially powerful teaching tool.

If we can avoid the controversy of good and bad in regard to videos, then we can look at them for their educational potential. Because videos are self-motivating for students, they can become highly successful instructional materials in the classroom.

To begin with, videos can be used for analysis. Recorded videos provide us with a visual representation of music that can be stopped, frozen in time, and manipulated. A good educational introduction to videos would be to juxtapose two videos, one from each end of a long continuum. This continuum has at one end videos that depict or elaborate the lyrics of a song. At the other end of the spectrum are videos that depict the musical characteristics of the song. One can find examples of videos from just about anywhere along this continuum. The two I would like to play for you are "Leave It" by Yes and "Pink

Houses" by John Cougar Mellencamp. "Leave It" depicts the music while "Pink Houses" depicts the lyrics.

Once your students watch these two videos they can discuss the differences. This is an important activity because the two ends of this spectrum are not new to the world of music. The lyric and music ends of the spectrum correspond to two traditional philosophical schools of musical thought: the absolutist and the referentialist. Having students debate the difference between these two schools can lead to many interesting and worthwhile class discussions that can rival those of many graduate classes in both content and excitement.

Once the difference between these two approaches is perceived, try to focus classwork on the type of videos that depict *musical* characteristics.

The next logical area of study is to analyze how the video captures the musical characteristics of the song. Discussion I have had with classes has revolved around identifying instruments that are playing a part highlighted by some visual techniques, or finding where in the music the visual scenes change. Classes have also been able to "observe" modulations, harmonic accents, and harmonic tension created through the use of pedal tones. Students were able to "see" form and meter when they discovered that scenes usually change on the first beat of a measure and that major subject changes in the visuals occur when a new part of the form appears (for example, at the start of a verse or chorus).

Some musical discoveries are made independently from the teacher. While analyzing the Yes video described previously, a high school class discovered that the visual scenes consistently correspond with four-bar musical phrases. With that one discovery, the students realized the importance of phrasing!

At this point, the students will almost certainly want to *make* their own video. Encourage this desire because videos are not hard to produce. Simply follow these simple steps:

1. Choose a piece of music. Try to find one that has many musical contrasts and is interesting to the students. Be sure that the students have never seen a video of the chosen song, for having done so will make it difficult for them to be original.

2. Create a graphic representation of the piece. A timeline in seconds works well. The graph should depict major sections of the music.

3. Decide what musical characteristics are to be highlighted and denote their location on the graph.

4. Decide how the selected characteristics will be highlighted visually.

5. Film the video.

An important item to remember is that the emphasis should be on the *process* of making the video, not on the end result or product that is the video itself. Classroom videos will never look as good as professionally prepared videos; however, if the emphasis is on the process, educational goals will be served. School orchestras should not be criticized because they do not sound as good as professional orchestras; so too for the classroom music video.

Classroom video in practice

Although I first started making videos with high school students, I have since been invited to several junior high and elementary classrooms to help students create videos. I have yet to see a class not excited about the prospect of making a video. I have always been impressed by the creativity students exhibit as well as the hard work they are willing to contribute. Their insights into the music are significant. Making a video brings out the best efforts of young people.

Since an article I wrote about making videos appeared in the *Music Educators Journal* some time ago, I have received numerous letters from teachers who have tried the procedure. All of those who have written have experienced the same type of success I have described. Recently, a teacher from Montana sent me a tape of videos that her elementary classes had made. She explained that after the students make these tapes, a committee, including the school principal and the janitor, chooses the best one. The winning production team wins a trip to Billings, Montana, for a pizza party.

Obviously, I am not the only music teacher enjoying the benefits of using videos in the classroom. Perhaps you, too, can employ this process with high school general music classes.

The future

Rock music appears to be entering what might be called its third major phase: that of digital or synthesized music. This is an exciting, evolutionary era for music. The new compositional technique that is emerging is that of the stratified rhythm sound predominant in the traditional music of many non-Western cultures. This technique is easy to capture in a visual form simply by building layers of visuals or increasing the complexity or movement of visuals. From this vantage point, one could progress into the musics of many different cultures. Such an understanding would be a great introduction to a broader unit on world music. A song that would work well for this purpose would be "Take Me Home" by Phil Collins.

Inherent in this kind of presentation is the fact that many individual songs will be dated in a year or two. This is the curse of using current popular music. However, like the music itself, videos are here to stay. They will change as the music changes. It is to our benefit to accept them as teaching tools. It is also imperative that we become knowledgeable about them so we can follow their growth in the years ahead.

Teacher Training for High School General Music Instruction: The Methods Class

by Richard O'Hearn

Introduction

This workshop session was presented in three parts. The opening segment addressed essential goals for the secondary school music teacher training program and methods classes. A model methods teaching sequence followed as the second segment. It was designed to elicit discussion from conference participants and from students from the University of Central Florida and Florida State University who served as the demonstration methods class. The final segment included a discussion of what did or should have occurred in the teaching sequence. This report is a summary of the goals of the proposed methods class model and the pertinent discussion points developed from the teaching sequence.

Goals of the training program

Before we teach secondary school general music methods classes, it is important to establish general goals for preparing secondary school music educators. The paramount goal should be developing a commitment to the concept of general music at the secondary level. In the broadest sense, this means recognizing the characteristics and interests of nonperformance-oriented high school students. The secondary school curriculum should move beyond the usual emphasis on performance classes and theory and music appreciation courses. To accomplish such a goal, the teacher education program should stress the notion that performance is only one means for learning; applied performance skills are not the only indication of a person's musicality.

Teacher education courses should help future music teachers acknowledge that some individuals place value and meaning on nonperformance modes of musical experience. These nonperformance modes may include such things as going to concerts, collecting and listening to recordings, and viewing music videos.

Secondary school music teacher training programs should assist prospective music educators in developing all forms of musical behavior. Performing, describing, and creating or improvising

76

should be used with equal skill and enthusiasm as teaching tools. These behaviors are viable, accessible ways of experiencing music. Prospective music teachers should cultivate their abilities to identify and demonstrate appropriate instructional techniques that use all three ways of interacting with music. In addition, the total program should seek to develop the ability of preservice teachers to exhibit valuing behaviors that reflect personal beliefs about the purpose of music and music education in order to make musical and instructional decisions.

Goals of the secondary school music methods class

One of the essential goals of the general music methods class should be to develop new values in prospective teachers. One such value is a belief that the core of the secondary school music curriculum should include courses in which description becomes the prime musical response. Description may occur through dance and movement, verbal and written responses, drawing, and other such activities. These activities should be viewed as the primary means for extending the descriptive competencies of the student; they are closely related to the performance application skills used in the general music class.

The primary focus of the methods class should be on developing specific teaching skills and understandings that help learners extend descriptive behaviors. Such a focus should encourage developing an attitude whereby the future teacher finds that teaching students to be perceptive listeners is as satisfying an instructional experience as is teaching them to perform. The resulting satisfaction may be even greater if the teacher views the development of perceptive listening as a partnership process between the student and the teacher. In order to feel successful, the teacher will need to value small changes and increments of growth, and then develop ways of communicating to students that growth has occurred.

Another goal of the secondary school methods class should be cultivating the concept that all individuals need opportunities to engage in musical behaviors of their preference. The future general music teacher should value high school students' ideas and suggestions about the general music class and its activities. This valuing process may result in joint evaluation and articulation of new, more interesting ways to strengthen course content. Student input may include suggesting study materials and class activities.

To further interaction, the methods class should help future music teachers to acknowledge that good music exists for all styles, places, and periods; therefore, a wide variety of quality music is available to meet the needs, interests, and goals of both the college methods students and high school general music students.

Developing musical behaviors is an important goal of the methods class. Musical behaviors fall into three general categories:

describing, performing, and creating or improvising. Descriptive behaviors include applying personal knowledge in analyzing compositions both aurally and visually. Descriptive behaviors also include using this knowledge to identify essential or unique characteristics of specific works as potential objectives for teaching strategies. The challenge for the music teacher includes moving the student into a formal thinking process. In formal thinking, the high school student learns to use a vocabulary of words, movements, gestures, and visual representations to describe music in meaningful ways.

The methods class should also promote developing prospective teachers' personal performance skills as a means for demonstrating musical examples. In order to become more fluent in stimulating creative musical behaviors, the methods class should seek to develop teachers who can compose and improvise musical patterns to illustrate specific compositional devices.

Listening to music should not be treated as an isolated event in the methods class, but as a model integrating all activities occurring in any music classroom. Whether describing, creating or improvising, or performing, students at any level always should use and develop their perceptual listening skills. The stimulus that dictates all learning activity is usually the sound of recorded music or musical examples that are performed in class.

Instructional goals for a methods class should include developing teacher competence in anticipating problems through techniques of task analysis and then determining the appropriate or needed focus of classroom activity. It is essential for the methods class to foster developing alternative strategies for use with different levels of cognitive skills, learning styles, and musical behaviors.

The class should attempt to develop teachers who, when planning instructional strategies, ask themselves questions about their students. Are the students at an "experiencing" level of interaction with music? Are the students at a "translative" level of interaction? Do they need to use nonmusical symbols or icons to depict their musical understanding? Can the students express themselves through the use of music symbols, either verbal or written? Do the students need instruction that incorporates more than one cognitive skill level in order to succeed? In terms of learning styles, do the students learn best from visual, kinesthetic, or aural strategies? Will students benefit from a mix of these presentation styles to bring about learning? Which musical behaviors meet the needs, skills, and interests of these students? Do the students need more than one musical behavior to develop musical understanding?

The methods class should seek to develop teachers who can match strategies to an individual's learning style, learning "set," personal goals, and current level of accomplishment. Finally, it should be a goal of the class to develop teachers who sequence classroom activities and experiences so that the learner can move from a known, through an unknown, to a new known.

The model class

The model methods class proposed here requires a partnership between the school music teacher, the college music education professor, and the college student. When possible, it is important that the college student observe the school music teacher, the college music education professor, and peers actually working in the real setting of a high school general music classroom. The goals of such partnerships should be to develop flexible and imaginative thinking and an openness to a variety of teaching models. These goals should encourage developing ways to change or vary the planned lesson process in order to meet the music education needs of high school students.

The variety of models observed in both the campus and high school classrooms should promote critical thinking as well as an openness to student input that can be used in the classroom agenda of both settings. Since there are teaching processes and procedures to be established in the methods class, both the school music teacher and college music education professor should identify ways of implementing these procedures in order to encourage the teaching style and personality of the individual college student.

The proposed methods model requires closely supervised field experience. It is important that the first few weeks of the methods course contain intensive observation and study of learning styles, cognitive levels of understanding, learning goals of the high school student, and teaching styles and procedures that are encountered both in the campus and high school setting. To develop these skills, the methods class should present both the right and wrong ways of doing things, followed by discussion questions such as: (a) What worked well in this class? (b) What did not work and needs to be changed? (c) Might each methods student implement or adapt the basic process involved? (d) How might the lesson be structured to reach all levels of cognitive development? and (e) How might the instructional materials be presented so that they correspond to the learning styles of the high school students?

The college methods professor should initiate class discussion that could lead to growth in critical, analytical, or imaginative thinking. The goal of the class model is to develop teachers who are sensitive to individual needs and who perceptively understand why a given way of implementing a lesson plan works well for one teacher and fails for another. Most important, while the model stresses thorough lesson planning, the lesson plan itself is viewed only as an outline that helps the teacher focus, modify, and deliver instruction; learning to vary the plan as needed clearly ranks high among the responsibilities of all classroom teachers.

Discussion topics

The methods class sequence led to discussion of the following issues:

1. The need to address all cognitive levels of understanding when teaching and reacting to the music

2. The need to use a variety of musical behaviors that meet the needs and goals of all high school students enrolled in a general music class

3. The need to have a lesson sequence that begins with music, focuses on the problem to be studied, and ends with music

4. The need to include all learning styles when implementing the lesson plan

5. The need for the stimulus (music) to relate to the interests and goals of the high school students: Music that is contemporary or that reflects students' subcultures may facilitate more immediate student involvement

6. The need for the teacher always to model good musicianship in all musical activity—whether playing dictation drills or performing a melodic example

7. The need for the methods teacher to be receptive to ideas and constructive criticism. This should lead to the same kind of openness by the methods students. These students should develop the ability to recognize why a teaching strategy works or falters. They should be willing to adjust a strategy to their own personal teaching style and use suggestions for improving their presentation style and sequence.

8. The need for probing questions to get the college students to evaluate critically whether the cognitive level, learning style, musical behaviors, stimulus materials, or concept focus is appropriate for the students enrolled in a given high school class

9. The need to treat a lesson plan as the framework upon which the teacher improvises to meet the needs, interests, and goals of the high school students

10. The need for continuous, positive, critical evaluation of the lesson plan and teaching models among the teacher and students in the methods class: The class should foster an atmosphere of respect, sharing, openness, and adaptability among all participants.

Part V:

Curriculum Models for Secondary General Music

Music Perspectives: A Component of an Arts Requirement for High School Graduation in the Baltimore County Public Schools

by Michael Jothen

A minimum of one credit, earned through a full year of study in the arts, is required for graduation from high school in the Baltimore County Public Schools, Towson, Maryland. This credit is earned upon completing two classes: Art Seminar and Music Perspectives.

Art Seminar focuses on in-depth study of the visual and plastic arts. The class is one semester in length and provides all students with half a graduation credit.

An additional half-credit toward graduation is provided all non-performing students upon completing the Music Perspectives course. This one-semester course aims at providing participants with a broad-based "perspective" regarding music and its historical development. Selected content from Music Perspectives also is presented to students in major performing ensembles. In this manner, members of performing ensembles earn a half-credit through a full year's participation in a performing ensemble.

The content of Music Perspectives

The focus of instruction in Music Perspectives is based on experiencing, examining, and evaluating the characteristics and qualities of eleven diverse musical compositions. Each has been selected for its potential to provide students with an expanded view of music. Emphasis is placed on assisting students in developing an awareness and understanding of music history, different compositional procedures, and the varying styles of musical expression available to the music consumer.

At present, the compositions included in Music Perspectives are:

Toccata and Fugue in D minor, Johann Sebastian Bach
Messiah, George Frideric Handel
Don Giovanni, Wolfgang Amadeus Mozart
Symphony No. 5, Ludwig van Beethoven
Overture 1812, Peter Tchaikovsky
Prelude to an Afternoon of a Faun, Claude Debussy
The Rite of Spring, Igor Stravinsky

Variations on America, Charles Ives
Rodeo, Aaron Copland
West Side Story, Leonard Bernstein

Selected works representative of Black musical style are also included. In addition, three supplementary compositions are available as options within the formal curriculum. These are:

Concerto in D minor, Wolfgang Amadeus Mozart
Claire de Lune, Claude Debussy
Fourth of July, Charles Ives

A curriculum guide emphasizes these compositions as the basis for instruction, course content, and instructional procedures. Outlines for lessons, units, and instructional packages are contained within the guide. These are based on the musical concepts derived from each composition; the historical, social, and cultural background relating to each composition and its composer; and the potential relevance of each composition for the consumer of music.

Curriculum objectives

For each composition the guide presents numerous instructional objectives. These are based on recommendations from the MENC publication, *The School Music Program: Description and Standards.* Within each objective, emphasis is placed on involving students in the music studied through varying combinations of performing, describing, and organizing. Specifically, students are asked to develop and extend skills in:

Performing (producing musical sound)
  1. Using the body as a musical instrument
  2. Using the voice
  3. Manipulating environmental sound sources
  4. Playing instruments

Describing (responding to musical sound)
  1. Listening to music and demonstrating understanding through:
    a. fundamental movement or expressive dance
    b. visual representation, including diagrams and abstract drawings
    c. verbal description, including both image and technical terms
    d. the use of traditional and nontraditional notational systems
  2. Reading music:
    a. translating the score into sound
    b. verbal description, including both image and technical terms

Organizing (creating music through determining the sequence of musical sounds)
  1. Developing of musical ideas through improvisation
  2. Communicating one's musical intent through composition or arrangement

84

Teachers are encouraged to plan, develop, implement, and revise lessons based upon suggestions and materials contained in the *Music Perspectives* curriculum guide. As a result, methods and procedures for instruction vary from teacher to teacher and school to school. In one setting, a more performance-oriented approach might be used to direct instruction toward a particular composition. In another, a discussion emphasis might be more appropriate. Most instructional settings find teachers using a balance between performing, describing, and organizing.

To assist in the process of developing instructional materials, the curriculum guide provides suggestions for a variety of different settings. Included are "music perspectives in performing classes" and "a lesson plan suitable for slow learners." These serve to provide assistance in developing lessons that meet the needs of students.

In addition to traditional classroom instruction, a symphony concert is a part of the Music Perspectives experience. Once each semester the Baltimore Symphony Orchestra presents a concert. Each concert consists of works contained either in the Music Perspectives curriculum or a combination of these plus other works by the same composers.

For some students, this concert experience marks their first opportunity to attend a symphonic concert. For others, it might be a regular activity. All students attend the concert with prior knowledge of most of the compositions and all of the composers. Both teachers and students are encouraged to view this experience as an extension of the classroom.

Developing Music Perspectives

The Baltimore County Public Schools have a K-12 student population numbering approximately eighty-five thousand. These students are served by 250 instrumental and vocal music specialists. At the elementary school level (grades one through five), students are provided twice weekly with classroom vocal music instruction. In addition, at the fourth-grade level, all students take instrumental "exploratory" music for one additional period per week. Formal elective instrumental instruction meets twice a week beginning at fifth-grade.

Middle school students (sixth through eighth grade) are required to take music two or three times per week for each year depending upon their grade level. Each student may elect to participate in either general music, orchestra, band, or chorus.

Senior high school students (ninth through twelfth grade) may elect to participate in both large and small group instrumental and vocal performing ensembles. In addition, courses such as music theory, keyboard, guitar, and musical theater may be elected by interested students. As in most high schools, however, the majority of students elected not to participate in music course offerings.

The option to *elect* high school experiences in the fine arts changed in the fall of 1983. Since that time, senior high school students have been *required* to enroll in Music Perspectives. This requirement came about as a result of a county study group begun in 1980. At that time a high school committee was formed to examine requirements for graduation. In 1982 this committee recommended more stringent graduation requirements including a course in fine arts. Gradually, the requirement emerged as one full credit in the arts, rather than one course in fine arts. This credit was to be divided equally between art and music.

Developing a course to fulfill the music component of the fine arts requirement was begun during the 1982-83 school year. The Baltimore County Public Schools have had a long tradition of summer curriculum workshops. Throughout the spring and summer of 1983, music teaching staff, supervisors, and the coordinator of music education were involved in identifying and reviewing options for a course that would meet the fine arts requirement. Existing nonperformance-oriented courses were examined and found to be inappropriate for a variety of reasons. Performance-emphasis classes were also considered to hold limited appeal for the general student population.

Given the strong tradition of general music in the elementary and middle school, students not currently interested in participating in existing music offerings might be attracted to a course that offers a modified general music approach. However, such a course must be different from those at the lower levels. Yet, it could build upon and use prior course learnings and experiences as a basis for developing content and instructional approaches.

The initial draft of the *Music Perspectives* curriculum guide resulted from the 1983 summer curriculum workshop. This guide was used on a pilot basis in all high schools during the 1983-84 school year. In-service courses were provided throughout the year to assist performance-oriented teachers in developing classroom teaching techniques. Vocal and instrumental teachers were supplemented by full-time Music Perspectives teachers in several schools. Throughout the school year, teachers, administrators, students, supervisors, and parents were encouraged to provide comments and suggestions regarding this course.

In the summer of 1984, the *Music Perspectives* curriculum guide was revised. Using the comments collected during the previous school year, teachers and supervisors revised the contents of the guide. Since that time, minor changes and additions have been made. In addition, future curriculum changes are anticipated in such areas as (a) altering "core" compositions to reflect changes in student and teaching populations as well as cultural conditions; (b) modifying activities to address the varied needs of higher and lower ability level students as well as the varied age and grade-level groupings; (c) including additional materials of a multicultural nature; and (d) expanding the literature lists currently suggested for use with performing ensembles.

Reaction to Music Perspectives

Music Perspectives has been in the curriculum of the Baltimore County Public Schools for the past four years. Throughout this time, comments and suggestions have been made regarding many aspects of the course. Initial reactions from both teachers and students tended to center on "Why do we have to do this?" Gradually, however, students, teachers, parents, and administrators have come to respond to the intent and purpose of this course in a very positive manner. It is not unusual to hear comments such as:

"This music is really great. Thanks for sharing it with me."

"It has brought a new dimension to my teaching."

"I didn't like any of this music when this class started. Now, it's OK."

"This has really revitalized me!"

In a relatively short period of time, Music Perspectives has become an integral part of the curriculum of the Baltimore County Public Schools. Through the process of encouraging reflection on the nature of a music program at the senior high school level, this course has helped draw attention to the process of education in music. It has been and I hope will continue to be a challenging and rewarding experience for both students and teachers.

A Humanities Approach to High School Music Courses in the Fulton County, Georgia Schools

by Joanna Rainey

"World Studies 500." Is this an unlikely course title for a strong presentation in creative aspects of the humanities? Not at all. Is it a course that would never attract many students? Wrong.

World Studies 500 ("Creativity") is one of the most popular elective courses for seniors in four high schools in Fulton County, Georgia. It had its beginning in December 1984 as the result of a chance meeting of two longtime friends, Charlotte Spungin and Joanna Rainey. In a discussion that involved catching up on fifteen years, Charlotte Spungin, teacher of psychology and head of the Department of Social Studies at South Broward High School, Hollywood, Florida, described an exciting project in which she had been involved. She was chosen to write with Tom Cicero a curriculum guide for the documentary television series, "Creativity with Bill Moyers."

The curriculum guide is built around the sixteen videotapes from the television series. The guide for each program includes a program summary, a profile (if the subject is an individual), previews and selected quotations, spelling and vocabulary words, entertainment and learning activities, a bibliography, and ratings (tests). The videotapes are titled:

"A Portrait of Maya Angelou"
"Olympics of the Mind"
"Samson Raphaelson"
"The Investors"
"Pinchas Zukerman and the St. Paul Chamber Orchestra"
"Painter/Sculptor/Welder Gerald Scheck"
"John Huston"
"NCAR (National Center for Atmospheric Research)"
"Out Art"
"Norman Lear Part I: The Creative Process"
"Norman Lear Part II: The Creative Person"
"Garbage—A New Way of Seeing"

"The Photographer's Eye"
"That's No Tomato—That's a Work of Art"
"Fred Smith and Federal Express"
"Women and Creativity"
"High School for the Performing Arts"

The primary focus of the course is creativity in its many manifestations. The curriculum guides and videotapes are used as vehicles to stimulate the sensitivity and imagination of students and teachers. The curriculum includes magazine and newspaper articles, books, theater, museums, businesses, concerts, and local persons who have used their creative spark to broaden and extend their professional and personal lives. Through all these resources, students are encouraged to explore and expand their thought processes.

Developing the World Studies 500 curriculum

A study of the curriculum guide in Fulton County prompted contact with the social studies curriculum director, Helen Richardson, who read it and responded enthusiastically. Both the social studies and music departments had long been concerned that students not generally attracted to performing arts courses should have an opportunity to experience "a moment of freedom"—a chance to take advantage of the unexpected, the indescribable flash of awareness, the aesthetic conundrum. The time seemed exactly right to move toward a new venture. Much dialogue between the social studies and the music departments followed. Ideas began to develop and the design of a course involving art, drama, music, and social studies came into focus.

After presenting the idea to the curriculum directors of these departments, the next step was to schedule an appointment with the associate superintendent of instruction. A full presentation of a possible course with accompanying logistical plans was enthusiastically received by the associate superintendent, who gave his permission to prepare for implementation. Four high schools were selected whose principals would be willing to "take a risk" and whose faculties included art, drama, music, and social studies teachers who were creative, imaginative, dynamic, sensitive and perceptive and who could work together in a team at each school.

The timeline on organization was an important factor. In February 1985 multiple copies of the curriculum guide "Creativity with Bill Moyers" were ordered. The plan was presented to a system humanities committee; principals of the four elected high schools were contacted, and a more detailed outline was developed. The next step in the planning process involved ordering the videotapes of the Bill Moyers series. This purchase was funded jointly by the five departments cooperating in the project—art, drama and English, media services, music, and social studies.

In May 1985 Spungin, who had been a source of continuous support, encouragement, and information, was invited to conduct an intensive two-day workshop for the sixteen teachers. These teachers had been identified during the spring, and their participation was confirmed immediately after the opening of school. Coordinators of all departments involved were excited about the possibility of this class; they each contributed time, energy, and budget allocations to the success of the venture.

The workshop for teachers, who would begin teaching the course for the first time in the winter quarter 1986, was offered in September. Supply teachers were scheduled, and all curriculum departments were involved in organizing this important in-service training. Because the choice of location for the workshop was an important factor, it was decided that a spot somewhat more aesthetically appealing than a high school gym would be desirable. Arrangements were made to hold the two-day workshop in the Members Room at the Atlanta Historical Society (AHS), John Ott, director of the AHS, and his entire staff were most cooperative and made the entire complex available to teachers and staff. During breaks the teachers were given the opportunity to visit the museum, the library, and buildings within the complex. The end of the workshop left teachers and administrators consumed with excitement.

An early decision to use the course title "Creativity" was changed. An old humanities course, recently retitled "World Studies 500," was still in our board-approved high school catalog of courses, but was seldom taught. The use of this title would enable us to offer the course as soon as we wished. World Studies 500 was entered on the computer printout as a course offering for winter quarter. The enthusiasm of the teams in each school subsequently stimulated large class enrollments. As hoped, students were delighted with the course, and subsequent quarters have found seniors eager to enroll.

Expanding the program

Plans in Fulton County call for World Studies 500 to be taught in the four selected high school for two years. These schools are in different geographical locations, and each has a different student population profile. The original plan was to fieldtest the course for two years and then to offer a staff development course for teachers in other schools to which the program might be expanded; it is hoped that this plan can be followed.

Questions have arisen particularly about the feasibility of expansion. Although response to this course has been enthusiastic, the venture has not been without problems. Everyone who has taught World Studies 500 has expressed difficulty and doubt about the grading process. The question is the same: "How do you grade *creativity*?" One workable suggestion is that a point system be used (100 points per week or 100 points per topic) so that teachers have the flexibility of grading more on effort than on ability.

In June 1986 a curriculum committee met and outlined a course built around the television tapes and guide. They also incorporated activities, and strategies and suggested materials based on the experiences of the teachers who taught the course in the preceding winter and spring quarters. This guide is now a part of the official curriculum of the Fulton County School District.

In conclusion, I would like to share with you some of Bill Moyers's guiding ideas about creativity. Perhaps his thoughts may help to stimulate similar curriculum development for your high school music courses.

> Creativity is about awareness of variance and novelty, keeping ourselves open to seeing things in a new way. Of course, not everything novel is creative. Nor is every product, nor is all intensity of energy, nor all learning, nor all change. Something may be new but trivial. To be creative, it must prove itself by generating significant insight, insight that changes our attitude and behavior.

> To be creative, you have to take risks, question what other people take for granted, look at the familiar in a brand new way, seize luck as it passes, use your imagination, and allow your unconscious to use you. (Spungin & Cicero, 1984)

References
Spungin C., & Cicero, T. (1984). *Creativity with Bill Moyers: The curriculum guide.* New York: Corporation for Entertainment and Learning.

Appendix:

Conference Participants

Conference Participants

Arizona
Brandom, Marilyn...Flagstaff
Pursell, Penny..Flagstaff

California
Ulrich, Frances S. ....Northridge

Colorado
Besack, Larry..Greeley

Connecticut
Modugno, Anne D. ....Stamford

Florida
Arnett, Patricia..Miami
Bell, Clark...Boca Raton
Berger, Roxanne G. ....Clearwater
Boyle, David..Coral Gables
Brown, Amy...Tallahassee
Choice, Norman...Lake City
Dorman, Phyllis...Gainesville
Fague, Alice...Orlando
Fullerton, Shelby...Bradenton
Harlacher, Charlene..Orlando
Hinckley, June...Tallahassee
Hoffer, Charles R. ....Gainesville
Hughes, Jane...Tallahassee
Hughes, William..Tallahassee
McCrary, Brenda...Orlando
Neff, Patty ....Orlando
Nefflen, Mary...Spring Hill
Palmer, Mary...Orlando
Rang, Julia ....Orlando
Robinson, Russell...Gainesville
Rowe, Velma...St. Petersburg
Ruggles, Carolyn ....Orlando
Smith, Bobbie ....Tallahassee
Smith, Dave..Ormond Beach
Stafford, Donald..Tallahassee
Strong, William...Tallahassee
Toler, Kimberly...Tallahassee
Trice, Patricia ....Tallahassee

Georgia

Dlouhy, Susan M. ....Atlanta
Gingrich, Donald..Atlanta
Monsour, Sally ....Atlanta
Rainey, Joanna..Atlanta
Shull, Suzanne ....Atlanta
Taebel, Donald..Atlanta
Walker, Charles C. ....Columbus
Woodard, Diane..Riverdale

Indiana

Waite, Barbara ....Evansville

Kansas

Haack, Paul..Lawrence

Maine

Grindel, Susan B. ....Orono

Maryland

Jothen, Michael ....Towson
Mollard, Sid ....Rockville
Silverstein, Rebecca..Baltimore

Massachusetts

Smith, Marsha Kindall ....Newton Centre

Michigan

Datz, Ruth E. ....Ann Arbor
Dolliver, Barbara ....Bloomfield Hills
Lehman, Paul ....Ann Arbor
Lehman, Ruth..Ann Arbor
O'Hearn, Richard..Kalamazoo
Palmieri, Valieri ....Bloomfield Hills
Snyder, Bruce..Bloomfield Hills

Minnesota

Kiester, Gloria ....Northfield

Missouri

Van Zee, Norma..Warrensburg

New Jersey

Distefano, Dan ....Ridgefield Park
Harper, Tyson ....Morristown
Moore, Janet L.S. ....Piscataway
Policastro, Joan..Whitehouse Station

New York

Bearss, Joyce...Glens Falls
Halter, Kim Jon.. Rochester
Lobaugh, Jimmie B. ....Rochester
Muro, Don ....Freeport
Neuen, Sue..Rochester
Phipps, Nathaniel J. ....Albany
Pogonowski, Lenore...New York
Windes, Patti...New York

Ohio

Cutietta, Robert A. ....Kent
Gerber, Timothy ....Columbus
Lauterbach, Charles W. ....Cincinnati
Metz, Donald ....Cincinnati

Pennsylvania

Conte, Jim...Newtown Square
Sims, Edward R. ....Slippery Rock

Tennessee

Crowe, Carey C. ....Knoxville
Crowe, Mrs. Carey C. ....Knoxville

Texas

March, Hunter ....Austin

Utah

Glenn, Avery ....Salt Lake City
Kenney, Susan ....Sandy

Virginia

Anson, David G. ....Newport News
King, Phyllis B. ....Herndon
Yeager, John ....Richmond

Wisconsin

Wolf, Richard W. ....Madison

1015-1M-02-1/88